The Road to Equity:
The Five C's to Construct an Equitable Classroom

The Road to Equity:
The Five C's to Construct an Equitable Classroom

Kayren Gray, M.Ed.

Andrea Hall, Editor

The Road to Equity

www.mkresultsllc.com

Be a Barrier Breaker

MK Results, LLC.
2020

The Road to Equity:
The Five C's to Construct an Equitable Classroom

MK Results, LLC

First Printing: 2020

Publishing Editor: Andrea Hall

Contributors: Andrea Hall and Danielle Guillory

Facebook Page: @mkresultsllc
Facebook Group: /beabarrierbreaker
LinkedIn: /kayrengraymkresults

Website: www.mkresultsllc.com
Email: kayren@mkresultsllc.com

ISBN 978-1-7349867-0-9 (Paperback)
ISBN 978-1-7349867-1-6 (Hardback)
ISBN 978-1-7349867-2-3 (eBook)

Dedication

This book is dedicated to all those whose story in education has been underrepresented, silenced, ignored, or assumed.

We **hear** you.

This book is dedicated to all the educators who not only believe all students can succeed, but put it into practice every single day by checking self at the door.

We **see** you.

This book is dedicated to all those who connected with my experience in some way or another – whether as a student, parent, educator, administrator, or advocate.

We **feel** you.

This book is dedicated to all the stories waiting to be told, shared experiences that create human connections – beyond the barriers.

#shareyourstory

#barrierbreakers

#closethegap

#theroadtoequity

Table of Contents

The Road to Equity

Acknowledgements

To my mother, Georgia, a phenomenal woman, who believed in me as a child and as a result, I learned to believe in myself. For this, I am forever indebted and only hope to replicate the same belief, in students and leaders, with each encounter.

Thanks, Mom.
Love always,
Kayren
#TheGoldenChild

Foreword

The Coronavirus was the catalyst that illuminated the social inequities that were steeped in the shadows of public indifference. This information about social inequities is not new. Education and social advocates have offered empirical data that specify how these systems of social inequities have adversely affected African-American, K-12 students through the education assessments and disciplinary processes. This research is ominous regarding the education outcomes and experiences for this group of students. It is unfortunate that these systems of inequities are fostered in a culture that is infused in the pedagogy of the American classroom.

If the Achievement and Opportunity Gaps are going to be dis-mantled, educators and administrators will need to reevaluate how they engage students in the multi-racial/ethnic/cultural classrooms. It will also require a knowledge and understanding of implicit biases and how they can influence how a learner is perceived.

To assist in making a difference and changing the trajectory regarding educational inequities, Kayren Gray has developed a resource, The Road to Equity: The Five C's to Construct an Equitable Classroom. This practical and powerful workbook will empower the reader to understand their role in dismantling the barriers that influence negative education outcomes and illustrate how to advocate for a fair and equitable educational process. Kayren's masterful use of Maslow's Hierarchy of Needs is marvelous, as she offers practical strategies that can mitigate inequities and ensure students have a transformative educational process that will enable learners to achieve their full potential!

Reverend Philemon Brown, MBA

"Research shows when kids see themselves

In books and see themselves represented;

they allow their trajectory to be like what they see.

You can't be what you can't see for the most part."

– Rev. Philemon Brown

Philemon Brown is a former Organizational Diversity and Development staff member at The University of Texas at Austin who currently serves on the board of Community Hands, a non-profit focused on providing resources for youth and family development, higher education preparation, elderly advocacy, and wellness.

"Not everything that is faced can be changed,
but nothing can be changed until it is faced."
James Baldwin

The Road to Equity

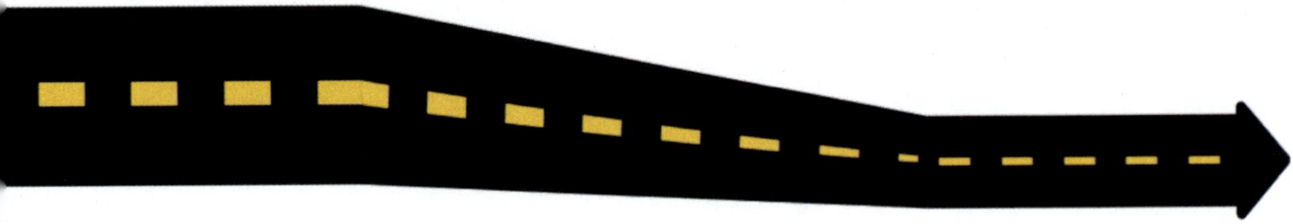

Preface

Steve Jobs said, "Your work is going to fill a large part of your life, and the only way to be truly satisfied is to do what you believe is great work." I knew my life had purpose, but I did not fully come to understand what Mr. Jobs meant until I entered education and looked many of my *own* conflictions in the mirror. I came face-to-face, seeing myself in my work, and I was not sure if it had always been this way or if I was just becoming more aware of it. My lesson started here, learning, first, that it is not *what* we do, but *why* we do, what we do that fuels the heart of every organization.

It was 1993, and I was six-years-old. I remember my mom and dad corralling my siblings and I, all, into one bedroom of our suburban home, asking us to take a seat on the bed. The time was early afternoon, and the sun rays were beaming through the window blinds – giving light and silently calling to me, a hopeful first-grader who loved nothing but to play outdoors. Giddy from school activities and with playtime in sight, all five girls settled on the edge of the queen-sized bed, with mom and dad standing near. What proceeded was what would turn out to be a life-changing conversation that included words and phrases like: "It is not your fault," "We love each other, still, very much," "Things will be different," and somehow the entire conversation ended with the single word, "Divorce." Each of us dealt with the fallout in our own ways. Nevertheless, at that very moment, I was impatient and simply ready to get back to the fresh air of the fall, not realizing just how much of a roadblock this would be for me, later on.

When I reflect on my public education experience, I smile fondly at the childhood I am grateful to have been afforded, despite barriers and circumstances. I smile fondly at those *few* educators who saw through my wide and bright, brown eyes and extended love enough to cover most of the bumps that life had already given me. I smile fondly at the educators who judged me on "the content of my character," and looked pass "the color of my skin", as proclaimed by Dr. Martin Luther King, Jr.

However, as an educator, when I reflect on my K-12 public education and the juxtaposition of my experience, as a student, versus my experience as a teacher, I am *conflicted*. I frown on the number of times I felt uncomfortable and alone, hearing staff and students make racist and/or ignorant comments about one or the other. I frown, looking back on the time that I tried out for the cheer squad and made the team, wondering if I was selected because of the *quota* for minorities that *had* to be met, or did they *really* pick me, for me? I frown, thinking about the times I looked away from injustice and blatant inequalities and discriminations, in education, because *they* were not treating "*me*" differently. I frown at how many times I shrank myself to become invisible, out of fear of *standing out* even more than my skin and being labeled as "that person..." I frown at the nights I stayed up confused on curriculum, studying late hours with no outlet or resource to support and enrich my learning. I frown for that *once* bright light that was eventually dimmed in me, an innocent child, now exhausted from simply trying to keep up with it all, foreshadowing to the "imposter syndrome" that would later haunt me as an adult: Am I worth it? Was I worthy? Does what I say matter? These are all the questions that the *conflicted* me would ask to, well, the *conflicted* me...

I grew up in a town where *few* looked like me. Our single mother worked two to three jobs to ensure that she could afford to pay for extra-curriculars, and because she felt too prideful for government assistance, she worked those jobs like she *had* to and without complaint. To add weight to an already heavy load, my mother did not receive consistent child support from our father. In the years following my parents' divorce, I began to understand the stress and strain of the circumstances that were undoubtedly beyond my control. What was really concerning is just how much I could actually *feel* the pain of it all, even as a kid. Looking for a place where I could find some type of comfort, school was my hope for an outlet to drown out the dream of what *could* have been for our family, had the divorce not actually happened. But that dream would become an illusion, instead — clouded by the many activities I was involved in: my close friends, sibling antics, and my personal academic goals, fueled by the notion that success would be my *best revenge*...And for me, it was, and even if reality said it wasn't, for me, it was, and that became the numbing, yet motivating *salve* that I longed for and so desperately needed to soothe the *wounds* of that aforementioned pain...

At a young age, I began to understand and see pass the smile on my mother's face that, in actuality, translated into pain. I was intuitive, curious, and observant. This was a gift and a curse — another thing to add to the baggage I carried with me to school. I *felt*, what other people at school—students and adults—were saying, without them having to *really* say anything, at all. I *felt*, when other people at school looked at me differently or shifted when I entered the room, intuitive enough to hear their repulsive comments, still, without them having to *really say* them, at all. I could only imagine what happiness felt like, when I saw the smiles and kindness shown towards certain people (opposite of me) and longed to be *that kind* of "normal." I wanted to replicate it in my own life—unaware of what I know now—nothing was wrong with me, but something was wrong with the people who treated a six-year-old differently, as if I had asked for and even deserved the things that made me *"unique"*, in my eyes, but just plain *"different"* in *theirs*... It is true what Maya Angelo said all those years ago, "I've learned that people will forget what you said, people will forget what you *did*, but people will never forget how you *made them feel*."

As a student...

As a student, in my graduating class of 152, there were only 13 African-American (8.6%), 5 Hispanic (3.3%), 132 Caucasian (86.8%), and 2 Native-American (1.3%) students. In the school staff, the numbers were even less diverse and a lot more dismal: 0.4% African-

American, 4.1% Hispanic, 95.5 % Caucasian, and comprised of 36.9% males and 63.1% females (Source: Texas Education Agency, Academic Excellence Indicator System, 2005-06 Performance Report). My resources were limited and access slim, as nothing surrounding me seemed to represent or reflect who I was, at all. Becoming a quiet, self-proclaimed chameleon, I quickly learned and felt that no one appeared to show any concern about my future beyond high school. Looking around, I observed how people who looked *different from me*, dealt with people who looked like me and different from *them*; ultimately, I learned that how people treated you depended on a number of circumstances—race, socio-economic status, parents' marital status, and so much more. Again, I longed to be "normal" in a world where I was an outcast – whether asked about my hair or how "different" I was; why my nose looked like this; why my skin scarred darker; why I talked the way that I did. "Why was [I] so *different*?" was always their question, and why it seemed to matter so much was always *mine*.

As a student, this experience left me feeling like the *only* champion for myself and my future, besides, of course, my mother, was *me*. On the flip side, as an educator, I reflected on this experience and wondered how many other students were their own *only* cheerleader or champion in school, as well. Isn't school supposed to be a place where you can learn, grow, and develop your skills? Yet, to feel so isolated at school, where education leaders spend countless numbers of hours on "vision and mission statements" geared towards student connectedness and student success, only to *still* have students walking hallways and sitting in classrooms feeling like no one cares about them or their future is such a tragic disservice and utter disgrace—especially since school is one of life's greatest influencers for who we are and all that we will become. Did they not care? Did they not know what to say or how to say it? Had they ever been taught or even interacted with people who were contrasting to their own identity?...And by "they", I mean my teachers, who were so different from me, and even my peers too...Had they not been taught or mastered the ability to coexist and constructively function and operate with those who were different from them? It is sad, but it is a hard truth that I asked, even at a young age and find myself asking and seeking to answer to this very day.

I struggled to define my self-worth in a world where no one looked like me or nurtured my differences as a positive. My story, as a student, is one defined by perseverance, despite the challenges and social inequities. But I often think back to what it would have felt like if schools were a place of positivity, confidence-building, growth, and a place where students *actually* develop mindsets of success. What opportunities would I have been extended, made accessible to, or even exposed to, if my school experience afforded me the same energy it extended to my peer counterparts?

As a parent...

As a parent, the conflictions I dealt with as a student manifested themselves in a new area. On May 23, 2006, at 9:28 p.m., I gave birth to my own bundle of joy, who would later enter kindergarten like most students—eager, excited, and apprehensive. I remember praying for him before he was even born; not just for the tangible and, of course, the norms, but I prayed for him to be successful, kind, compassionate, and just. What I did not realize, in raising a son, was that there were challenges of which I was never aware—the challenges faced, in education, by young men of color. I did not realize that the roadblocks encountered in my son's educational journey would open my eyes to another systemic issue plaguing our educational system. The Band-Aids I used to cover my own wounds were a temporary fix to processing my own experience; however, those Band-Aids were being ripped off slowly, as my own son had *his* own enemy of biases to encounter and stereotypes to dispel. I felt the mistreatment, as my son would innocently explain his day and sometimes question why certain kids received this or that, but he did not. It was hard to explain all of this to my child, an innocent kid, because I was still nursing my own wounds from school; however, the mirror of my past, now, appeared so very presently and chipping away at my son's own sense of self. This is a child who, again, asked for nothing but to be afforded the same opportunity to learn. The same extended courtesy I gave to many other parents as a teacher of *their* children, I expected the same reciprocity for my own son, but did not always get it. Yet, I felt trapped - crippled with fear and paralyzed by a system I was working in, but was not working for me. I felt the unequal distribution of harsher discipline to my own child. I witnessed *lower* expectations, from educators, being placed on my child, to his disadvantage, *and*, at the same time, *higher* expectations, from educators, being placed on my child, *also* to his disadvantage—all because of the color of his skin. I felt the belittlement of fellow educators and principals towards me, his mother, via communication and in person, not valuing my concerns and even being subject to their stereotypes.

As an educator...

As an educator, and more specifically a social studies teacher, I knew the power I possessed as a black, professional female, delivering culturally-relevant lessons in which all students could connect with and see themselves. I knew the responsibility I had to share the stories of historical figures, and, at the same time, allow my students to share *their* stories – stories that brought meaning to their life, motivation to cover their defeats and barriers, and inspiration for them to break those barriers and overcome roadblocks. While serving as the lead teacher of the social studies department, I thought about my responsibility to ensure equity, differentiation, and representation in the curriculum in order to help students understand the impact of history. My own experience became the catalyst to fuel my innovative, welcoming, and inclusive classroom. I worked in high schools whose student demographics were far more diverse than my own high school. Entering public education nearly a decade ago, my focus was to share my own passion for learning with others and ultimately, impact the lives of students who felt that history—or school for that matter—was not for them. I soon realized and began to understand how important it was and *is* for students of color to see success in people who look like them, providing them with an example and a "roadmap to success." In fact, when students see success in people who look like them, their own success becomes more attainable and far more real. By building meaningful relationships and making learning culturally-relevant, I vowed to equip my students with, not just content, but skills they can utilize beyond school and in the real world.

As an administrator...

As an administrator, I, again, was faced with a glaring image of myself in the work. I knew a coping mechanism for myself, as a student, was to become engaged in the arts, groups, sports, and academics—all provided by school. I wanted to ensure students felt like they belonged to school, hoping that this could be as much of an outlet for them as it had been for me. I wanted to create a platform where student voices were valued and their interests taken to heart. One of my principal leaders was feverishly passionate about student-connectedness. My interest peaked, as my own personal story connected to him, as a leader, and to his mission for the school. Helping collect research and seeing my own story in the work, I started my master's program, and, through my research, I identified a positive correlation between student engagement and student academic achievement. As a student activities coordinator, I wanted every students' voice to feel empowered and heard, opposite of my own experience. I connected with those kids who were silent, not because they did not have anything to say, but because they believed no one cared to hear it. Those were walls I wanted to see come tumbling down as a leader.

Just like my classroom, I wanted those that entered my office to feel welcomed, valued, and loved. In addition, building relationships proved most valuable, not only with students, but with colleagues, who were vital in helping to facilitate the translation of the mission from mere words into action. Club sponsors *were royalty* in my book. They truly possessed the patience, humor, and nurturing spirit needed to grow our students through shared interests, fostering a sense of belonging. Anime? Guitar? Poetry? Kindness? There was a club, sport, or event for each student to find "their people." Even from my own high school experience and now working in one, I saw the same type of students being selected to be representatives, picked for opportunities, or selected to speak, causing me to form and institute more inclusive school initiatives and practices, across **all** student activities. I wanted active student engagement and participation from a host of different students, where a broad spectrum of ideas and input could be considered, not just the ideas and input from the *typical* and same *few*.

In April 2019, while working at a phenomenal Early College High School (ECHS), recognized, by Educate Texas, as a model College and Career Readiness School, teamwork and flexibility were legends on the map, helping provide a sense of direction and collective mindset to shift the paradigm. The program, instituted by the state, was established as another alternative pathway to success for at-risk students to obtain their high school diploma and associate's degree upon graduation. It was truly revolutionary, but required innovative minds and team collaboration to fulfill the goal. Taking eighth graders and transitioning them to *high school* (let alone college), was no easy feat, and yet this transition to college was exactly what we did at ECHS. Nevertheless, the collaboration and effort of our visionaries and administrators, met by our campus educators and counselors, was instrumental in making what was a mere vision years ago—a reality, and, in May 2019, the first graduating class of ECHS represented a monumental milestone, becoming trailblazers on this new path to success for students.

Through my experiences, as an administrator, the inequities were evident in schools, whether it was funding, lack of resources, policies, etc. It was here, where I found myself *yet again*, faced with conflictions, inequitable practices, and systemic policies, coupled with the barriers limiting how wide *my* impact could be. This time, I leaned on the wise words of Gandhi, "Be the change that you wish to see in the world," and I did everything that I could to be that change.

As an advocate...

As an advocate, I have encountered more stories with students that are similar to my own—students *still* walking toward their future with uncertainty, lack of self-confidence, and anything but self-assured about the next few years ahead. I longed for options, exposure, opportunities, access, equity, equality, diversity, inclusion, and quality leadership. Was that too much to ask? Aren't *all* students deserving or just some? How can we ensure no student is left behind?

The result...

The issues clogged my mind like five o'clock traffic on Interstate 35, bumper-to-bumper, with more construction than the law should allow, and no visible end or solution in sight. It reminded me of a long drive home – familiar yet uncanny, and sometimes wondering how you got there, not remembering or conscious of each turn or stop that you made along the way. My story was like the track on the cassette, but with the button stuck on repeat. The louder I tried to drown out the music, it got louder – so loud that I could no longer drown out or ignore what I must address. What became even more apparent was the frightful realization of this reality: "the same direction **_will_** produce the same result," prompting drastic measures, on my behalf. My experience, to some degree or another, in each role: student, parent, and administrator, was showing up in various parts of my daily life. Faced with a choice, I decided to no longer look away, assume the problem would fix itself (after all, I have been out of school for fifteen years and the same issues were still present), or focus on another teaching strategy to close the gap. I was tired of shrinking myself, viewing failures for "some" students as normalized behavior, and wanted to find a way to heal and prevent reoccurrences. Education was *not* in my rear-view mirror; education remained the focus and forefront of all that I did, but a new approach was ignited— advocacy. As a result, I decided to partner with other courageous educators who also seek to advocate for voices too often underrepresented, silenced, ignored, or assumed.

MK Results, LLC

Refer to **Appendix H** entitled "The Road to Equity"
to understand **equality, diversity, inclusion,**
and why **_equity_** *is* necessary.

Introduction

*"Every single person you will ever meet
shares that common desire. They want
to know: do you see me, do you hear me,
does what I say mean anything to you?"*
Oprah Winfrey

The purpose of *The Road to Equity: The Five C's to Construct an Equitable Classroom* is to provide best practices as tools to better understand equity and close the achievement gap. I selected a road because it signifies a journey of getting from one place to another, a movement of progress in the right direction. The intention is for educators to use the Five C's as a road map that leads to a more equitable classroom, producing more equitable outcomes, yet, truthfully, some of these same principles can be applied and render themselves effective within any organization. Each chapter is a story and a stop along the road, with application and reflection as you travel towards educational equity.

What is Equity?

Each student is deserving of an equal opportunity to learn. An understanding of equity is necessary, if equality *is* the end goal. **Equity means giving each person what they need in order to reach success.** Equity *breeds* equality. When educators and leaders are provided with clear guidance on equity expectations, they can better provide their students with access to a pathway towards success. In this year, 2020, there has been a shift in the state-driven emphasis on education, which no longer focuses solely on college-readiness, but college, career, and military readiness—representing multiple pathways to success (even more than I had myself).

So, if we are being honest, and this is my intention for sharing my story, I am willing to be vulnerable, so that other educators have the courage to do the same. With that said, I am willing to break the ice, confront that huge "elephant in the room," and just flat-out ask one of the toughest questions that no one wants to ask: **When it comes to equity, are all students truly presented with equal and fair opportunities?** Do they truly have access to all of the possible pathways, leading to their success, or does their zip code dictate the pathways that are available to them? We must see and hear the stories of our students, in order to better assist them on their personal path to success. However, when we examine the education gap that exists across America, failure is much more accessible, normalized, and presented as an *opportunity* than success. It can be daunting, frustrating, and damn-near impossible to change the educational system overnight, a system engrained in tradition. Instead, we challenge the mindset of leaders to shift the heart of the system.

- In education, the term *"equity"* refers to the principle of *fairness*. While it is often used interchangeably with the related principle of *equality*, equity is a little different, as it encompasses so much more.
- *Equity* is a wide variety of educational models, programs, and strategies that may be considered fair, but not necessarily equal.
- Think about it this way: While a "**process**" is:
  - *how* something gets done;
  - the *manner* in which a task is completed;
  - the *method* by which an idea is actualized.
- An "outcome" is *what* you get when the process is completed.
- Therefore, it has been said that "**equity** is the process (*how* you get to a level and just playing field); **equality** is the outcome, (*what* you get once the playing field is actually leveled)."

The abovementioned principles are true, given that equity— what is fair and just—may not, in the process of educating students, reflect strict equality—what is applied, allocated, and distributed equally (The Glossary of Education Reform).

- AVID is a remarkable program, equipping students with preparation for college, careers, and life. They are known for providing access and exposure to students who will be first-generation college students. AVID, or "Advancement via Individual Determination", defines equity as "the *measure* of achievement, fairness, and opportunity in education."

- According to Bradley Scott (2000), the goals of schools are to produce "high student outcomes for all learners, regardless of race, gender, national origin, linguistic status, and economic status. If they are not, they may be good, but they are not excellent. After all, good schools have always worked for some students. The real issue is making schools work for **all** students."

If we want positive student outcomes and to change the narrative, educators must include the story of their students in their content, matched with effort from leaders willing to shift away from "the way things have always been" because *that way* is no longer working for *all* students.

This book calls for that shift to take place with immediacy.

What is at stake?

Identify

"*People without accurate information cannot act responsibly. People **with** accurate information feel compelled to act responsibly.*"
Blanchard, Carlos, & Randolph,
***Empowerment Takes More than A Minute* (2001).**

If we do not address this within our profession, we leave each educator and leader open to *personally* define what is fair, just, and equal, based on their own backgrounds and life-experiences. One of the DuFour PLC Essential Questions ask, "If learning is the goal for schools, how do we respond when students do *not* learn?"

The Texas Education Agency's 2019 Accountability Manual evaluates the performance of Texas public schools. "Closing the Gaps" (one of the domains that the Accountability Manual assesses) uses disaggregated data to demonstrate differentials among racial/ethnic groups, socioeconomic backgrounds, and other factors. The indicators included in this domain, as well as the domain's construction, align the state's accountability system and with the federal accountability system found in the "Every Student Succeeds Act (ESSA)." Within the state's accountability system, there are fourteen student groups identified in the domain, "Closing the Gaps." I have included the list on the following page so that you can identify what the state of Texas evaluates. Nevertheless, I have also inserted a few additional ideas and statistics to serve as "eye-opening food-for-thought," because, let's face it, whether we want to admit it or not, a *genuine* discussion on "equity in education," would *have to* extend to gender, sexual orientation, and other bias that are typically ingrained in thoughts – so natural, we often forget how they manifest themselves within the classroom – implicitly or explicitly.

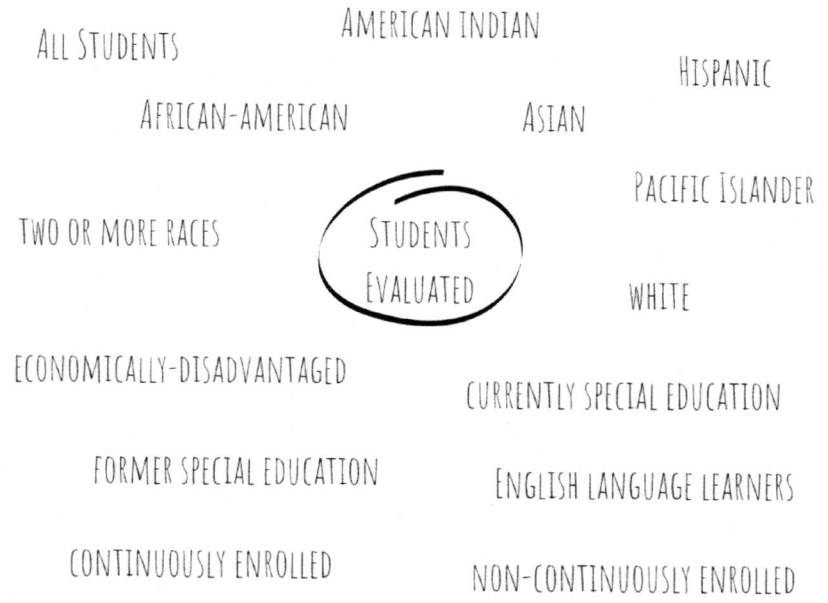

ALL STUDENTS   AMERICAN INDIAN   HISPANIC

AFRICAN-AMERICAN   ASIAN

PACIFIC ISLANDER

TWO OR MORE RACES   STUDENTS EVALUATED   WHITE

ECONOMICALLY-DISADVANTAGED

CURRENTLY SPECIAL EDUCATION

FORMER SPECIAL EDUCATION   ENGLISH LANGUAGE LEARNERS

CONTINUOUSLY ENROLLED   NON-CONTINUOUSLY ENROLLED

Now, reflect on the data below, and consider how it makes you feel to know this, as well as the implications of the following realities:

- America's public schools serve nearly **51 million students**.

- The racial demographics for **teachers** in America report 80.1% White, 8.8% Hispanic, 6.7% Black, 2.3% Asian, 1.4% Two or more races, 0.4% American Indian/Alaska Native, 0.2% Native Hawaiian/Pacific Islander.

- As of 2019, the demographics for **students** across America are as follows: 48.2% white, 26.4% Hispanic, 15.3% black, Asian 5.1%, Two or more races 3.6%, American Indian/Alaska Native Students 0.4%.

- **The National Center for Education Statistics reports fewer than one out of 10 educators are black** (6.8%).

- ...When considering gender, in addition to race, we know that **black males make up** *only* **2% of the teaching workforce nationwide.**

- *The Educator's Handbook for Understanding and Closing Achievement Gaps,* by Joseph Murphy (2014) draws alarming conclusions from the data: **African-American and Latino high school** *seniors* **have mathematics and reading skills equivalent to the skills of an average white** *eighth* **grader.**

- Based on census data, **38.1 million people** live in poverty in America.

- The National Center for Children in Poverty reports **19% of children in the U.S. live in families that are considered officially** *poor.*

- **Child poverty rates are highest among black, Latino, and American-Indian children.**

- **One in six children in America live in poverty.**

- Between the 2017 and 2018 data, people aged **25 and older, without a high school diploma, was the only examined group to experience an increase in their poverty rate.**

- Data from the U.S. Department of Education, Office of Civil Rights (2014) reports **African-American students are suspended and expelled from school** at a rate *more* than three times as high as white students (16% versus 5%).

- **"African-American, Latino, and impoverished students attend schools with higher concentrations of first-year teachers than do white students.** This means that these students are being taught by teachers with limited years of experience and expertise, which *could* and more than likely *does* impact the quality of education that these students are receiving."

- National Center for Education Statistics (NCES) estimates that the elementary and secondary **student population will continue to become less white and more diverse.**

- **The public-school student population is projected to increase in diversity.** The National Center for Education Statistics (NCES) predicts that white students will represent 46% of public-school students in 2024, a *drop* from 51% of the student population in 2012.

- During the same 12-year timeframe, **the proportion of Hispanic and Asian/Pacific Islander students is projected to increase.**

- **Hispanic, public-school students are projected to represent 29% of total enrollment in 2024** (compared to 24% in 2012).

- **Pacific Islander and Asian students are projected to represent 6% of total enrollment in 2024** (compared to the 5% in 2012).

- By 2030, people of color will make up <u>more than half</u> of the total workforce.

- In the book, *Overcoming the Achievement Gap Trap: Liberating Mindsets to Effect Change,* Dr. Anthony Muhammad concludes, **"People typically do not expect much from those they do not view as favorable or capable, education is no exception."**

Pacer's National **Bullying** Prevention Center reports the following:

- "The reasons for being bullied reported most often by students include **physical appearance, race/ethnicity, gender, disability, religion, sexual orientation**" (National Center for Educational Statistics, 2019).

- "The percentages of individuals who have experienced cyberbullying at some point in their lifetimes have *more than doubled* (18% to 37%) from 2007-2019" (Patchin & Hinduia, 2019).

- "Students with **specific learning disabilities, autism spectrum disorder, emotional and behavior disorders, other health impairments, and speech or language impairments report *greater rates* of victimization than their peers without disabilities longitudinally and their victimization remains consistent over time**" (Rose & Gage, 2016).

- "23% of **African-American** students, 23% of **Caucasian** students, 16% of **Hispanic** students, and 7% of **Asian** students report being bullied at school" (National Center for Educational Statistics, 2019).

- "More than **one third** of adolescents reporting bullying, report **bias-based school bullying**" (Russell, Sinclair, Poteat, & Koenig, 2012).

- "**Race-related bullying** is significantly associated with **negative emotional and physical health effects**" (Rosenthal et al, 2013).

- "70.1% of **LGBTQ** students were **verbally bullied** (e.g., called names, threatened) in the past year because of their sexual orientation and 59.1% because of their **gender expression,** and 53.2% based on **gender**" (Kosciw, Greytak, Zongrone, Clark, & Truong, 2018).

This *has* to change...

Consider the following excerpts from *Culturally-Responsive Teaching: A Guide to Evidence-Based Practices for Teaching All Students Equitably*, as author Basha Krasnoff reveals how to cultivate culture and climate at schools for *all* students to learn:

- "**Addressing the unique needs of students from diverse backgrounds** is one of the major challenges facing public education today because many teachers are inadequately prepared with the relevant content knowledge, experience, and training" (Au, 2009; Cummins, 2007).

- "**Inadequate preparation** can create a cultural gap between teachers and students that limits the ability of educators to choose effective instructional practices and curricular materials" (Gay, 2010; Ladson-Billings, 2009).

- "**Research on curriculum and instructional practices has primarily focused on white, middle-class students,** while virtually ignoring the cultural and linguistic characteristics of diverse learners" (Orosco, 2010; Orosco & O'Connor, 2011).

- "The contrast in the demographic composition of educators and their students is reason for concern because **research shows that students' race, ethnicity, and cultural background significantly influences their achievement.** Therefore, the more students see educators who look a lot *less* like them, the greater the risks are for lower academic success and achievement" (Harry & Klingner, 2006; Orosco & Klingner, 2010; Skiba et al., 2011).

- "There is extensive evidence from achievement test scores, grade promotion rates, graduation rates, and other common indicators of school success that **students from culturally and linguistically diverse backgrounds experience poorer educational outcomes than their peers.** Additional factors, such as poverty and inadequate training or professional development opportunities for teachers, compound this negative impact, as do systemic issues like biased assessment practices and institutional racism" (Bennett et al., 2004; Conchas & Noguera, 2004; Sanders, 2000).

- "Disproportionate rates of <u>suspension and expulsion</u> **for students of color** result in a *substantial loss* of **instructional time.**"

- "The goal of equitable education is not to help students learn to adapt to the dominant culture of the school. Instead, the goal should be to **help students develop a positive self-image and to learn how to embrace differences in others**" (Ladson-Billings, 1995).

- "Therefore, teachers must be prepared with a thorough **understanding of the specific cultures of the students they teach; how that culture affects student learning behaviors; and how they can change classroom interactions and instruction to embrace the differences.**"

- "Reasonably, **teachers can only be held accountable for student outcomes** *if* they are <u>**adequately prepared**</u> to be culturally responsive to their students' learning styles and needs."

Nationwide research captures inequities and discrimination, continuing to highlight a larger "culture" gap in education. America's student demographics are becoming more diverse, while the makeup of educators remains stagnant. Fisher, Frey, and Hattie understand the process of equity in attaining equality. In *Developing Assessment-Capable Visible Learners, Grades K-12* (2018) the authors assess the heart of the system to begin the journey towards equity. "School systems must work in concert with students, teachers, and leaders to close the opportunity-to-learn gap. This requires a focus on issues of equity, which are addressed, in part, through the way we structure schools so that every child can become a visible learner."

Here is the point and motivation of this entire book and why we do what we do: **We have an educational pandemic occurring, largely ignored by the majority because it is not impacting their household directly.** However, disparities in academics remain a leading problem in education, leading to larger, long-term impacts and strains on communities and society. The gaps in education will leave students behind, unprepared for college, a career, or the military, widening the gap further and leaving the "left-behind" far more vulnerable and at a disadvantage. This disadvantage, experienced by the "left-behind", can and will be the same disadvantage that burdens society, overall, creating social issues, such as increased poverty, the need for more government assistance, heightened crime rates, and so much more. This is a disadvantage that I believe we all have a responsibility to collectively eradicate.

The disparity between the "haves and have-nots," the educationally "advantaged and the disadvantaged" is overwhelming, and after decades of *attempts* to change this, the results remain dismal and unchanged. Our educators are not in need of another teaching strategy for literacy or a *magic formula* to make students behave. What we are in need of is culturally-relevant pedagogy, infused with culturally-relevant learning experiences for all educators and students.

As an educator, myself, I was an expert in my subject-matter and content of social studies, but never received any training or knowledge on how to teach students from different races, backgrounds, life experiences, religion, and lifestyles that were far more different from my own. As an educator, my colleagues and I were deemed "experts" in our subject-matter, but it was often assumed everything else in the classroom would simply "fall into place." We knew "the **what**," some of my colleagues even knew "the **why**," but more of us were uncertain of "the *how*."

Implement

"As we work to improve skills in behavior management, we must assess three areas: our beliefs, our words, and our practices."
Dan St. Romain

We must identify the problem in order to implement a solution. If we *truly* believe every student can succeed, what does that sound like, and how might we need to adjust our practices to reflect our beliefs? The work requires deep and authentic reflections and conversations to close the gap. The chart below explains how one can *travel* "The Road to Equity" as an effective way to close the nation's achievement gap. Instituting equity and diversity training, focusing on financial literacy in school, developing strong and meaningful professional learning communities (PLCs), restorative discipline practices, and supporting social-emotional learning for students are all steps to be taken on this road that is presently *less traveled*, but must become the main *expressway, like Interstate 20, from the east to the west*, if we expect to truly close the achievement gap amongst the students of our nation. If we consider ways to understand, cultivate, and even correlate culture, currency, communities, and climate in all that we do, within the field of education (and within any organization, really), the achievement gap will begin to narrow. The use of data to drive instruction and next steps, will assists in understanding the breakdown in the classroom dynamics, as well as how — directly or indirectly—mindsets of adults can cause students to take *longer* routes, with far less access than their peers and counterparts, on their *road to success*, and could not only make for an excessively longer ride, but this factor, alone, could very well cause students to never arrive at the place of success that they seek, at all.

Consider the following chart as another road map on the journey to shift our schools to a whole child approach by addressing each area as a destination to close the achievement gap.

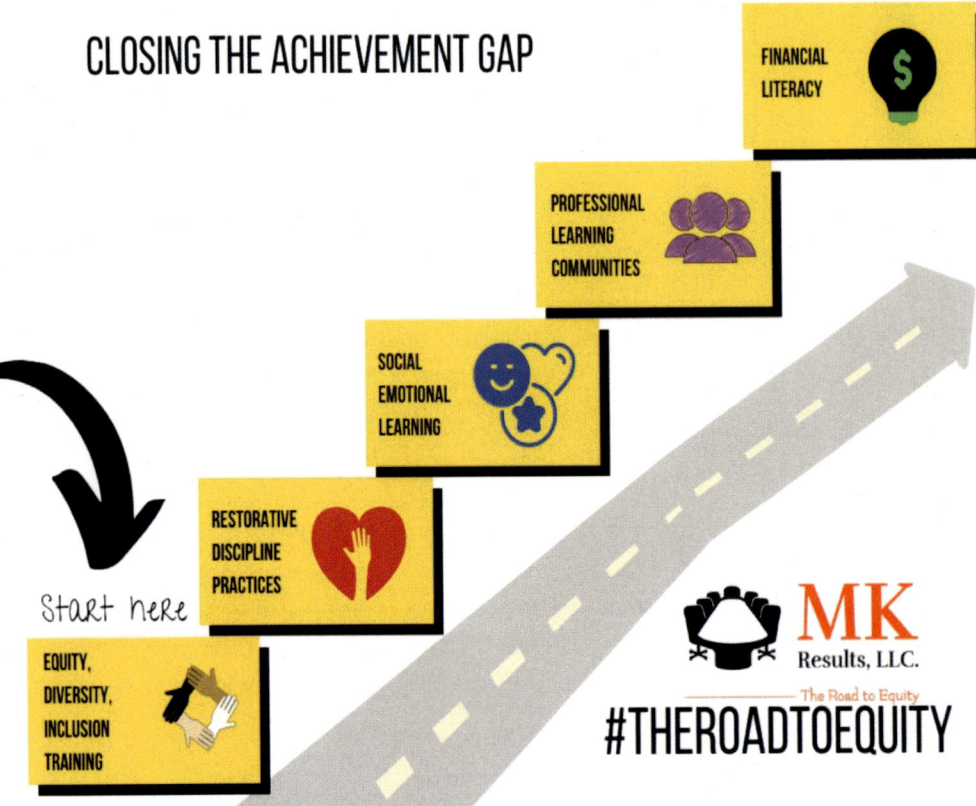

Along the trip, there are several ways to make traveling down "The Road to Equity" accessible for those that need support. Educators have tools at their disposal to implement and create real, quality changes. In this book, we will discuss best practices for an equitable classroom to ensure equitable outcomes. Our *biases* shape our world, our decisions, and our attitudes; the most important things to remember is that *everyone* has them. How do they show up in your classroom? Are you aware of how they directly or indirectly impact your students, shaping who they are and defining moments they will recall for a lifetime? We must collectively work together to dispel stereotypes, break down barriers, develop growth mindsets, and become more conscious of ourselves, in order to change the narrative.

We must begin "A Friendly Conversation" to set educators and leaders up for success, so they can do the same for our children. We must not shrink nor shy away from the truth revealed in qualitative and quantitative data. Again, the time is now to address "the elephant in the room" and for the *reflection in the mirror* (that means *you*) to share experiences that foster human connections. These conversations are part of the implementation process in a safe environment, in order to discuss issues of contention, privilege, and power necessary for change.

Sometimes the best conversations *are* the most uncomfortable – and that is where growth happens... understanding of shared experiences. It is not easy to discuss the realities facing our nation, our schools, our society; however, it is one that must be had in order to close the gap and change the narrative. If we shrink our experiences when others disagree or feel uncomfortable, we limit ourselves to share in other's pain, their story, their life experience. We deny, devalue, and deflect their story because the uncomfortable feeling is one, we have never experienced. I did not talk about race for a long time, or any issue for that matter—even if it did impact me directly, because it made *others* uncomfortable. In 2020, I am challenging myself and others to stand and speak up for injustice. No longer can we let our discomfort dictate the narrative. Start a conversation and #pullup at the table with an open heart.

Leaders must develop a comprehensive needs-based strategic plan to appropriately identify problems with research-based solutions and collaboration built on community and inclusion, leveraging our cultural differences as a resource to learn.

"A mandate for change requires that racially, ethnically, culturally, and linguistically diverse students have the opportunity to meet their learning challenges with the strength and relevance found in their own cultural frame of reference. Therefore, teachers must be prepared with a thorough understanding of the specific cultures of the students they teach; how that culture affects student learning behaviors; and how they can change classroom interactions and instruction to embrace the differences that exist among their students." –Basha Krasnoff

Inspire

"The growth mindset was intended to help close
the achievement gaps, **not** hide them."
Carol Dweck

Once identified, the solutions are implemented to inspire a collective effort to close the achievement gap when stakeholders are "all in." By fostering a new narrative in your community, you will begin to write your school's story on *The Road to Equity* defining the legacy of your district or campus and ultimately, you as an educator and leader.

Dr. Anthony Muhammad, author of *Overcoming the Achievement Gap Trap: Liberating Mindsets to Effect Change* stated, "After forty years of intensive research on school learning in the United States, as well as abroad, my major conclusion is: What *any* person in the world can learn, almost *all* persons can learn, if provided with the appropriate *prior and current* conditions of learning."

For a better resource and graphic explanation of the need for educational equity refer to **Appendix I: Why Equity?**

Why Equity?

The Road to Equity: The Five C's to Construct and Equitable Classroom and our "Closing the Gap" series, when implemented with fidelity, will boost the success of **_all_** students. In fact, the results will create:

- Increased attendance, academic achievement, confidence, and overall success of students, by providing them with a platform to be successful and productive citizens. The aforementioned results will also minimize disciplinary issues, creating more instructional time and positive interactions to support your students in meaningful ways.

- Pride, ownership, accountability, and a safe environment will be created throughout your campus or within your organization. This will equip people with the skills they need to solve problems with respect and communication, through "A Friendly Conversation", as the stakeholders begin to work as a team towards "The Road to Equity." The change will be noticeable in all interactions: student-to-student, student-to-teacher, employee-to-employee, employee-to-boss, boss-to-employee, employee-to-parent, and/or the employee-to-customer, etc.

- A decrease in discipline and classroom management issues, as educators are equipped to work towards closing the "culture" gap, by incorporating stories and out-of-text experiences that are either reflective of the teacher and/or representative of the student. Either way, the connection and rapport that educators will be able to build with their students, by closing the culture gap, will lend itself to a healthier and more constructive environment in which teachers can teach and students can learn.

If we truly believe "all *means* all," we must address ways to close the gap and find ways to ensure that all students are given what they need to be successful. This book is not a study of the root causes or debate on who is to blame; rather, it simply says that based on the data, a gap exists. It goes on to show that with this knowledge, here are tools that can be used to narrow the gap, hoping to eventually close it completely. From the sub-groups noted, and from my own experience, I, too, have had to take a stand and confront adult biases that penetrate to the core of learning. With the rapid changes in society and many circumstances beyond our control, again, I have developed a *road map* towards equity – ensuring the commitment that we all took when *entering* the profession, is one that we all *keep*, throughout it, even in the face of change.

MASLOW'S HIERARCHY OF NEEDS
Abraham Maslow
Motivation and Personality

THE ROAD TO EQUITY
Kayren Gray
The Five C's To Construct an Equitable Classroom

Self-Actualization — Celebrate

Esteem — Commit

Love and Belongingness — Collaborate

Safety — Create

Physiological — Confront

The Five C's to Construct an Equitable Classroom will revolutionize the perception of your students, classroom, campus, and district by providing a solution to close the gap and institute a more powerful, positive, purposeful message to be felt by those who are a part of your organization *and* those who are not.

The **detours** in my own life were the driving forces that led to a desire and mission to ensure educational equity. There were more **tolls** and **exits** I had to prepare for, while I observed others using **cruise** control and others being fortunate enough to take the **HOV lane.** Those moments in life that set me back or directed me to an exit, in order to refuel, changed a little piece of me—sometimes for the better, but sometimes for the worse. Those unexpected detours were my "North Star," shaping my experiences to prepare me to deliver a message that hopes to inspire you to do what you *can* to close the gap. In fact, if we all do what we can, little or much, it is *more* than we would see accomplished, if we all did *nothing* at all, and that is why this is so important to me.

My own story, as you will hear throughout the book, has helped to shape the workshops' topics and themes and has led to the formation of a collective team of like-minded educators with a vision to change the narrative, empower others, and be examples of embracing diversity. MK Results, LLC seeks to create a platform to facilitate a conversation on equity and to share a powerful message on the impact of unity, diversity, inclusion, and cultural competency that will *inspire* results.

Our commitment *must* be to promote diversity and inclusion among organizations, neighborhoods, jobs, schools, and communities because we expect upright, contributing members of society. In order to fulfill this, we must collectively prepare students **now** or we bear the burden collectively. We must help mold students to think critically in order to find the cure for a pandemic, ask questions in the face of injustice, and understand the value of their story as one worth telling and one that *is* a part of our nation's story.

By confronting our own inequities and biases, we are outwardly proclaiming to refuse to allow our differences to divide, isolate, and cause adverse reactions and behaviors. Rather, we proclaim as a collective, the time *is* now as the gap is continuing to widen.

Schools are foundational, community partnerships where students are introduced to social norms *and* academics – influencing outcomes for graduation, attendance, discipline, and ultimately their entire lives. Students are impacted positively and negatively from what goes on in the hallways, in classrooms, and on the field. We cannot always predict or control the behaviors of others, but what we can begin to shift is our contribution to perpetuating the narrative. The burden of campus climate and culture cannot fall on the students, *alone*, or the teachers, or the student council, it must be a *collective* effort to equip every stakeholder with the tools to understand biases and how they can unconsciously undermine our intentions and void our progress.

Symbolizing strength, courage, and leadership, I, Kayren Gray, am honored to share with you my journey of stepping out on faith and supporting communities to see real, quality change by partnering with other courageous educators, committed to *closing the gap*. If each educator makes a commitment to an equitable classroom, knowing the power they possess and impact they can make… imagine the results that would follow. Join us on #TheRoadToEquity, entitled a road because it must be traveled to get us to our destination – an equitable classroom. My hope is that you are able to recognize *roadblocks* and take preventive measures to avoid leaving any student behind. My hope is that this book serves as a tool, along the road, with the understanding, it takes application and that there is more work be done.

Utilize the *road map* to equitable outcomes, through my interpretation of "Maslow's Hierarchy of Needs," as a reference point, moving through each level to reach self-actualization or in our case, a more equitable classroom. Culturally-relevant pedagogy and culturally-responsive learning is the first pinpoint on our journey because, as the professionals, we cannot expect change from our students, if we do not first seek change within ourselves.

My hope is that this book helps everyone take a closer look at the varied human experiences that enter the doors of classrooms each day, carrying with them the weight and pressure of the world. Is it crazy to think that the power of one person, an educator, can brighten and lighten the load, bringing joy, encouragement, and kindness to all? No—it's not! How will your students recall their educational experience with you? I guarantee you; students will remember some of the content, but, like Oprah said, will most importantly remember how _you made them feel_. I believe every child is capable of learning, based on their ability, "but the *extent* of their learning is determined by their innate ability or aptitude" (DuFour, DuFour, and Eaker, 2002). I desire that every educator and leader join me in this belief. Above all, I desire that we, as educators and leaders, remember that we made a commitment to this profession, and part of that commitment is the belief that *every* child, that means <u>*all*</u> students, can learn and "all [irrefutably] means *all*."

Chapter 1: **Confront**

"Not everything that is faced can be changed,
but nothing can be changed until it is faced."
James Baldwin

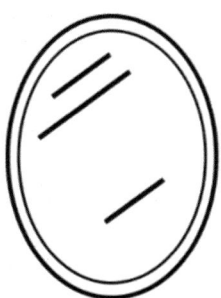

It was nearing the end of the semester around Christmas break; I received a phone call from my son's teacher. She proceeded to tell me how disrespectful my son was. She explained how she asked him numerous times to turn around in his desk; my son, a rather tall young man, stated he explained to the teacher he hurt his knee in athletics during first period and it was uncomfortable to turn in the small desk. He said he asked to go to the nurse twice, before she actually let him go, saying that the nurse would not be able to do anything for his knee besides an icepack. She had nothing positive to say throughout the entire conversation, but I assured her, nonetheless, I would address the situation.

A month later and into next semester, my son brought home an assignment to write a poem from a first-person perspective, in response to the event, "The Trail of Tears". The assignment was from the same teacher's class who had called earlier in the school year, about my son being "disrespectful." AJ explained that twenty-five extra-credit points would be assigned, if students "aged" their poem. As AJ got home from school, I asked him about his day and what he had to work on. He said he needed to use my computer to type his poem for class. He mentioned that he needed to age the assignment for extra credit and already had ideas on what he was going to do.

As a mother, I was excited that he was excited about the content he was studying and the product he was creating to express himself. As a novel, freelance, graphic design artist, I offered to teach and show AJ the cool technology features he could utilize to age his poem. We sat in our home office looking over antique designs, coffee stains, etc. We decided to print the poem on aged paper and added coffee stains, but the most memorable part of this project was the *grand finale*! The grand finale was one that, I'm sure, every person remembers doing at least once for a project, or at some point in theirs or their children's life, and, for us, it was when AJ burned the edges of his poem for the final step! He was proud of his work, and I was proud of his effort – seeing him motivated and getting it done was exciting and gratifying for both of us!

The day that AJ would submit his project, upon his arrival home from school, I asked him how everything went. Noticeably disappointed, he said that when he turned in his project, the teacher said it was *not* aged. I asked AJ what the criteria was, or if it was explained to them how the teacher expected the projects to be "aged." He said, "No." I asked what the other students' projects looked like, in comparison to his. From his adolescent perspective, he felt his project exhibited the same, if not *more* effort than his peers, who had received a response of approval from the teacher.

As a mother, I politely and respectfully emailed the teacher, asking what the criteria was for "aging" the assignment and if a rubric was available. The email received no response for *four* days. I followed up twice, assuming positive intentions, and as an educator myself, I know how much we have to balance, in addition to our own life circumstances. Nevertheless, as a parent, I did not want the issue to go overlooked, and it appear to the teacher that my son and I were *only* concerned about the grade because it was nearing the end of the grading period. I emailed the counselor, asking for her assistance with getting the teacher to respond. Within twenty minutes of the email to the counselor, the teacher responded to my email: "I gave AJ his poem back on Tuesday, after I read your email over the weekend. I thought he would have told you Tuesday evening."

After meeting with an administrator on campus, I felt heard, but then no real, resolution was made. The administrator conveyed to me the teacher said she could have him re-do the aging process again for the full extra-credit but she could only give him ten points for his attempt. I still have not had a rubric or explanation.

I emailed my concerns to the principal of the campus, outlining what unfolded and my disappointment. I never received a response or even acknowledgement of my concerns...

The Road to Equity

 *Eye on equity:*
Identify inequities
within the story

_____

_____

_____

_____

_____

Self-Actualization — **5** — Celebrate

Esteem — **4** — Commit

Love and Belongingness — **3** — Collaborate

Safety — **2** — Create

Physiological — **1** — Confront

Traffic Stop

In the model, above, "Confront" refers to the act of challenging your own perceptions, biases, and prejudices to foster self-awareness, and the first "C" in *The Five C's to Construct an Equitable Classroom* is to "Confront." Merriam-Webster defines the word confront: "To face, especially in challenge; to cause to meet; bring face-to-face." Closing the gap means understanding the barriers to learning, in order to "solve for Y." We must not look outwardly to see a change in the affects that bias and prejudices create, but we must be willing to confront and come face-to-face with ourselves, in order to see and be the change that we wish for. This is the highest form of reflection – confronting your own self in the mirror and coming face-to-face with hard truths. The key we must remember is that we are not alone. Every person, regardless of race, religion, culture, gender, etc., has a bias; no one is immune. We make quick judgments about other people, at times, based on what we see on the surface. This is a small glimpse of a person. (Refer to **Appendix B** for the "Cultural Iceberg.") Our schemas determine how we react and approach problems, conflicts, resolutions, and more, all based on each individual's life experiences and background. As we confront our own biases, we must reflect on how they manifest – implicitly and explicitly – through our actions, reinforcing or perpetuating stereotypes, without consciously knowing it.

Once you have identified your own personal biases, you can evaluate how, in the past, they may have and/or, in the present, may continue to manifest themselves in your life and in your classroom. This means – the choices you make, the procedures in place, the expectations – who are those set for? From whom, is the expectation derived? Do the procedures reflect equitable distribution of lessons and leadership? To understand your biases, take Harvard's unconscious biases test, entitled, "Harvard Implicit Association Test (IAT)," which has been presented through multiple platforms, such as Project Implicit's "Implicit Association Test (IAT)."

The link can be found in **Appendix A**. Reflect on the results, which address your personal, unconscious biases in order to determine areas to target. The assessment offers a *road map* to help you understand and most importantly, *reflect* on how those biases may directly or indirectly come out in your classroom, through your curriculum choices, grading practices, and view of some students (and even their parents).

Once you understand *how* your biases have directly or indirectly impacted your classroom, you can, now, understand the barriers to learning that many students encounter, which are vastly different from our own experiences. Taking yourself out of the equation and understanding that in the year, 2020, there are more circumstances that our children go through that are far more troubling than we have ever experienced. How unfortunate it is to live in a world where there are *more* resources at our disposal, and yet there are far more problems and issues caused by this plentitude than one could ever imagine. Unfortunately, more tragedies and lives are lost, *now*, than in our parents' generation. In fact, students feel more isolated and an increase in self-harm, all, stems from pressures experienced in social settings in school than ever before. Let's put that into perspective…

In Maslow's Hierarchy of Needs, the understanding is that one must satisfy the most basic needs, slowly ascending to ultimately reach their full potential, which is "self-actualization." *The Five C's to Construct an Equitable Classroom* is based on the same premise – educators must conquer each pillar in the pyramid, before moving to the next level and reaching the top or end goal – a more equitable classroom. The basis of Maslow's pyramid is physiological needs, such as food, water, reproduction, and clothing. These basic needs, for life to be sustained, are essential, as well as the motivating factors behind most behaviors.

When we identify our own way of thinking and how it impacts the classroom, we can begin to open ourselves up to viewing the world, as well as to understand the barriers facing our students, beyond their control, and impacting their learning. What we *can* control is *ourselves* and how we respond. We can identify our biases in order to alleviate one of the barriers that we can control, and that barrier is ourselves. The most important tool on this journey is **_reflection_**. The symbol for "**Confront**" is a mirror, asking you to look within *yourself* to address your *own* conflictions and challenges, in order to bring about change, growth, and awareness. The greatest challenge we face in life is usually the image we see staring back at us in the mirror. When we are ready to *confront* our truths, we begin to remove barriers along the roadway, giving ourselves and others access to better opportunities and more constructive interactions on their path to success.

Application

- Take the renowned "Implicit Association Test (IAT)" to become (more) aware of your biases.

- Create specific actions that you will take to practice overcoming personal biases that may be directly or indirectly impacting the learning of *at least* one student in your classroom.

- Find an accountability partner to embark on *The Road to Equity* with you. This is a person who believes in setting up all students for success, breaking barriers down to learning, *and* developing a growth mindset. We call these educators: Barrier Breakers! Find someone who challenges the status quo and who is willing to join you on an honest, authentic journey towards #TheRoadToEquity.

- Create a presentation of your story, including your background and path to education, and extend the opportunity for your students to join in and learn about who is the "responsible party" in the partnership of the student and teacher. Allow them to share in your willingness to be vulnerable. This may be a tough or challenging step, but, in turn, will help you *and* your students in the next pillar, as your students share who *they* are.

- Allow the space and opportunity to allow your students to discuss the barriers they encounter or face to help you better understand the challenges (especially outside of the classroom and many beyond their control) they must overcome to learn. Ask: What are some of the challenges you face in and out of the classroom? Be willing to listen without trying to fix or "solve for y," but be willing to reflect on how the barriers they express impact the learning of your students and at many times disproportionately.

Reflection

1. What is the purpose of equity, diversity, and inclusion in education and what does it mean in your classroom?

2. What barriers must you address consciously?

3. How might your biases manifest themselves in your everyday life, classroom, and the choices you make?

4. How have your *own* past and present life experiences shaped you?

5. What barriers must your student overcome to learn?

Case Study: Adultification Bias

https://www.law.georgetown.edu/news/research-confirms-that-black-girls-feel-the-sting-of-adultification-bias-identified-in-earlier-georgetown-law-study/

Tell your story

In the next chapter, you will learn how **confronting** your biases will *create* a safe and welcoming classroom, fostering connections between your students and others, their community, and the world!

Chapter 1 Notes: Confront

The Road to Equity

Chapter 2: *Create*

"Kids don't learn from people they don't like."
Rita Pearson

Leaving Pre-K was exciting, and I was ready to be a "big" kid, just like every other little person my age. At the start of my kindergarten year, I was apprehensive, curious, and thought that if Pre-K was this much fun, I knew next year, kindergarten would be even better! I *loved* learning and could not wait to soak in more. Writing letters in shaving cream, field trips, naps, and reading...all moments I think back with fond memories all while creating new friends and discovering my love learning.

However, my kinder experience became one that taught me many lessons as an innocent child- lessons that I should never have had to learn, especially at such a young age. Kindergarten was where I was introduced to differences and where it was made apparent just how different *I* was. My innocent little self, could not fully process or articulate what I was feeling or how it made me feel at the time because I realized it was better to blend in and remain unseen. So much so, I remember sitting for hours in soiled clothes, after an accident, fearful of my teacher's response and embarrassed at my inability to control myself, after asking to go to the bathroom and being told to "hold it."

Trying to process all of this, while watching my peers who looked *different* from me "ask and receive", without an issue or denial. Nonetheless, the experience snatched the light from my eyes and dimmed the sweet love I had for learning. In fact, my love for learning was overshadowed by my past experience, so much, that as I, now, sat in my new first-grade classroom, I wondered if I even had a shot this year. You see, Ms. Greene *looked* like my kindergarten teacher and my heart sank...another year of isolation, loneliness, and anxiety – better yet, another year of paying the high cost for being different.

Ms. Greene had long, thick, brown hair, a contagious smile, and I soon learned – a heart big enough for all her students. I was the age of six attempting to process the changes in my life, balance playtime, and learn to read. Feeling alone and uncertain, in a school and classroom, I found myself unable to focus. After all, it was as if life had changed almost instantly, when the word, "*divorce*", came out of my parents' mouths. Normal family routines were adjusted as my father moved out, and budgets were tightened, as a dual or double income was suddenly cut in half.

Being one of two little, *black* girls in the whole class, I was apprehensive about Ms. Greene, who was actually *white*, as were mostly everyone else in my class (with the exception of the other black girl and a Hispanic student or two). Moreover, for the first time in my life, sitting in this first-grade class, I wondered what horrific concept of race would be introduced to me, this year. I was apprehensive, especially considering my experience in kinder, where I learned that there is a cost for being *different* and an associating pain that comes from this thing called, "discrimination," before I knew or could truly understand what race and discrimination really was.

Nevertheless, and to my surprise, on this particular day, after coming in from recess and parting ways with my best friend, Katie, Ms. Greene kneeled down to my tiny desk and asked to talk to me at her desk. She quietly asked about my disposition and if there was anything she could do. She whispered to me gently that she heard my parents were going through a divorce and empathized with me.

Ms. Greene saw me and my circumstances, never judging but understanding how those barriers were indirectly impacting my studies. For the remainder of the year, Ms. Greene was the nurturing spirit I needed to restore my motivation, and she *created* a safe space to express what I was going through, even though I did not fully understand it. Towards the end of the school year, Ms. Greene stopped by my house and surprised me with a gift bag full of goodies – toys and candy – a *small* gesture with a huge impact that restored the confidence and joy back into the heart of that, now, seven-year-old.

The Road to Equity

STOP

Eye on equity:
Identify ways the educator
created opportunities to connect.
Compare/Contrast each grade-level experience

_____

_____

_____

_____

_____

Self-Actualization — **5** — Celebrate

Esteem — **4** — Commit

Love and Belongingness — **3** — Collaborate

Safety — **2** — Create

Physiological — **1** — Confront

Traffic Stop

Create refers to facilitating intentional opportunities between educator and students, with the purpose of seeking and finding a positive connection. Culturally-relevant teaching helps educators take into account the cultural backgrounds of students, in order to relate it to the content. *Create* opportunities to connect with your students to make learning culturally relevant and culturally responsive. The most fundamental tool at your disposal is your ability to foster, nurture, and maintain relationships. In *Under-Resourced Learners*, by Dr. Ruby Payne, she reveals that the primary motivation for learning, first, begins with the relationship. This is your secret weapon, most important ingredient, the first pit-stop on the trip, or *whatever* you choose to call it, to establishing a positive culture and climate in your classroom. As we are more aware and acknowledge our differences, the outcome is to be culturally responsive — appropriately and respectfully.

Educators are poised with a unique and timely challenge, along with the curriculum requirements, to build relationships and to connect with their students (now virtually). However, what does this look like to *create*, develop, nurture, and maintain said relationships? When working through a lens of equity, ***building relationships*** is where the exchange of ideas, knowledge, and perspective occur. When we examine our current school system, we find gaps in learning, an increase in disciplinary infractions, and a spike in attendance issues. We must remember that the data, although necessary to **confront**, is more than numbers, but also represents students hoping for a bright future to dream big. The issues we see and feel on campuses, across the nation, highlight the consequences of broken, failed, or non-existent relationships between *all* stakeholders: school, parent, educator, leadership, student, and community. We must work together collectively to address and identify the issues, implement solutions, and inspire results!

In Maslow's Hierarchy of Needs, our *"need for security and protection"* are the motivating factors to ensure safety. On "The Road to Equity," the educator has the responsibility to *create* opportunities for connections. This includes the curriculum, but before even getting to the curriculum, you must *create* opportunities for your students that make them feel safe to learn and participate in the learning. This act can be done in a variety of ways; however, be cautious to avoid stereotyping. Getting to know your students for who they are is important. Stereotypes perpetuate false narratives for a whole group and can lead to assumptions that could manifest themselves adversely when trying to genuinely get to know a person. Break the barrier of stereotypes by getting beneath the cultural iceberg and understanding that each student comes with a story, whether we can only see a portion (generally, when we first meet students) to discovering beneath the surface – characteristics that define their outlook and shape their life. You will discover what is beneath their cultural iceberg throughout the school year, but you must be intentional in creating those opportunities to truly reveal and understand who your students really are. In fact, you must genuinely find these opportunities to be just as necessary as progressing through your curriculum because, again, as Rita Pearson said, "Kids don't learn from people they don't like."

The goal is to be intentional in practices yet authentic in delivery, simultaneously. For example, at the start of the school year, set aside time to learn your students' story and what motivates them. By building meaningful relationships, students will respond best when they know the adult respects them and sees them as a person – their whole experience, not just the fifty-two minutes in the classroom, must be of the utmost importance. It is the same way we want our students to see us – as humans who make mistakes, learn, overcome, and most importantly, care.

As the educator, you are in the driver's seat, in charge of navigating students through your area of expertise (content and curriculum).

Students must, first, be willing to go on the ride with you by boarding the bus. However, what if some want to get on, but do not have the resources necessary; what will you do? How will you respond? This is where *inclusion* comes into play. Are you ensuring *all* your students have the opportunity to participate? Have you set *all* students up for success? Have you set out to **create** connections for all students to be involved or were your classroom opportunities created for only *some*? Each student and person for that matter – even you – have a story to tell. Former First Lady, Michelle Obama said it beautifully, "If we can open up a little more to each other and share our stories, our real stories, that's what breaks down barriers. But in order to do that, you have to believe your story has value." The role of the educator is to find creative ways to get students on board and provide an opportunity for them to share who they are, even if it means creating different approaches for different students, understanding their motivations, and listening to their narratives expressed through intentional engagement. Equitable leaders **create** a safe and nurturing classroom where students feel safe to express themselves – their voice – and one where students lift each other up. These same equitable leaders find value in all of their students' stories and would do whatever they could to **create** opportunities for their students to "open up a little more" each day. Despite our differences, we can still disagree or agree and respect and value other people. This all starts with the teacher being the facilitator of **creating** a culture where voice is valued. Once you have taken the time and effort to create a way for them to "board the bus", and they trust you in the driver's seat, students will begin to open themselves up to learning.

How do you make connections? James Comer summed it up: "No significant learning occurs without a significant relationship." Think back to the classes where you learned the most, what was your relationship like with the educator or coach? Through conversations and shared experiences, facilitated by the educator, students will discover connections with their teacher, their community, and society.

The role of the educator is to facilitate these opportunities by providing platforms of expression for students and help to dismantle biases that limit growth. Through positive examples and considering who is in your classroom, the educator is positioned to supplement learning by *creating* positive, cultural connections. By creating moments where educators have considered the *whole* student and their experience, educators will begin to build trust, as value is placed on *who* the students are, as well as their story. This means *creating* an opportunity for you to also share your own story with your students – humanizing the educator to be vulnerable and *creating* connections, as we are asking our students to do the same is one of the most profound and valuable experiences that an educator could ever create, and it's one that must not be omitted, as we travel this *"Road to Equity."* Robyn R. Jackson summarized what it means to know our students: "It means recognizing what currency they have and value, and then using that currency to help them acquire the capital of the classroom."

Refer to **Appendix C** for a complete examination of what equity looks like, feels like, and sounds like in your classroom.

Application

- Listen to your students' story. Listen to the message, not to respond, but to simply and genuinely hear *their* story. Students can replicate Maslow's Hierarchy of Needs with pictures for you to understand what *they* need in each area to reach their full potential. Use this as insight to your students' story.

- Have your students draw a picture of their family, in order to understand their home-life.

- Have individual, student conferences. Set aside time to do "temperature checks." This allows you to meet with students while they are working, individually, as a way to check in with them and them with you. This individual time allows you to check on their progress, and allow for space and time to continue to build a positive relationship. #TemperatureTuesday

- Use a "Personalized Index Card Inventory" or something similar to refer to when you are learning more about your students and to be referenced throughout the year. This quick reference will help generate conversation, understand your students' individual abilities and where they are, as well as the various circumstances that could impact their learning.

- Understand the strengths of your students to capitalize on their abilities – avoid prescribing traits to students based on what you see. There is more to everyone's story.

Reflection

1. How inclusive and attainable are your current classroom practices for *all* students?

2. What do your students <u>need</u> to feel safe enough to learn?

3. What actions or procedures must you put in practice to develop opportunities for connections?

4. Reflect: How do you think <u>*you*</u> connect with students who are different from you?

5. Compare what you define as a safe, welcoming, and inclusive environment/classroom to what your students need. Compare your responses to students who have similar backgrounds with you *and* those that are different from you. Identify and reflect on what they need in order to feel safe, to learn, and thrive while with you.

6. Do you devote time to building relationships in your classroom? Do your students believe you have a favorable or unfavorable perception of them and their cultural background? What would lead them to believe the latter?

Remember, our thoughts become our actions – what we see, becomes what we begin to believe, and impacts what we do, how we do it, and how *well* we do it with who...

Students tell their story!

What each person needs to feel safe is different. By getting to know your students, you understand what each student presents, both, in and out of the classroom, as well as what is necessary for them to feel protected and safe. Now that you have established opportunities for connections, the student becomes more involved in the process of collaboration, which will be discussed in the next chapter.

Chapter 2 Notes: Create

_____

_____

_____

_____

_____

_____

_____

_____

_____

_____

_____

_____

_____

_____

_____

_____

_____

Chapter 3: Collaborate

"When you know your WHY,
you can endure any HOW."
Victor Frankl

My favorite subject to teach was U.S. History. Having 11th graders, as my students, held a special place in my heart. I built relationships with my students and got to know them for who they were and what they brought to my class. The schools I taught at were predominately filled with students of color. Many students expressed, early on, the normal objections most history teachers hear: "Why do we have to learn this *old* stuff?" "This is *boring*!" "This has *nothing* to do with me." "History is just a bunch of dates to remember."

To me, juniors represented the second coming of age, as they crossed over to upper-classmen; with graduation so close, they could taste it, but they still possessed a combination of knowledge, curiosity, and enthusiasm. Freshman and sophomores were still giddy and immature, coming into themselves, as they navigated the still novel experience of high school. Seniors were focused on senior year things, like graduation, prom, and the next steps since it was so near, and oftentimes found it difficult to truly focus on the education matters that still weighed heavily on the difference between being a senior versus being a *"graduating* senior."

With juniors, it was as if time was standing still, just one more time before the rush of senior year took over. For juniors, their aura reminded me of the shiftiness between a baby and "big" kid – what you see in most four and five-year-old's, attempting to test out their independence, but still soft, impressionable, and willing to soak in all that you give – at the exact same time.

Anyway, when teaching the Civil Rights Movement each year, I made a point to spend specific days fostering discussions, viewing a documentary, and debriefing. To introduce the unit, I showed them a documentary, by PBS, on Emmitt Till, a fourteen-year old, black boy who was lynched in Mississippi in 1955, after being accused of making a "pass at a white woman." Students answered questions about the documentary. Emmitt Till represented many of my students – young, minority, and confused – with no outlet to ex- press or un- derstand the history or sacrifice endured. Moreover, Emmitt Till was fourteen, which was an age that all of my juniors could remember and relate to. The following Friday, I showed my students a video created by Teaching Tolerance entitled, "Children's March." The documentary showcases how students, with the youngest being four-years-old, got involved in the march for justice. Many students did not know how students their age mobilized behind an issue of equality and fair treatment for all. Students who were plummeted with water from fire hoses, bitten by attack dogs, and more; all because their parents could not share their story out of fear of losing their job and financial means for the family.

All of my students could connect with what it was like to be fourteen. My job was to paint the historical context for them to understand how different, yet similar their stories were, to each other, as well as to the historical icon that we were studying. My job was to defy their preconceived notions that "history [was] boring" and to dissolve their inhibitions, showing them that history had a lot to do with them- more than they may have realized, at first.

Nevertheless, my job would have been impossible, without a willingness to pull my students into the learning and 𝒸𝑜𝓁𝓁𝒶𝒷𝑜𝓇𝒶𝓉𝑒.

STOP

Eye on equity:
Identify collaborative efforts
within the story and/or ways
to be more collaborative - brainstorm.

_____

_____

_____

_____

_____

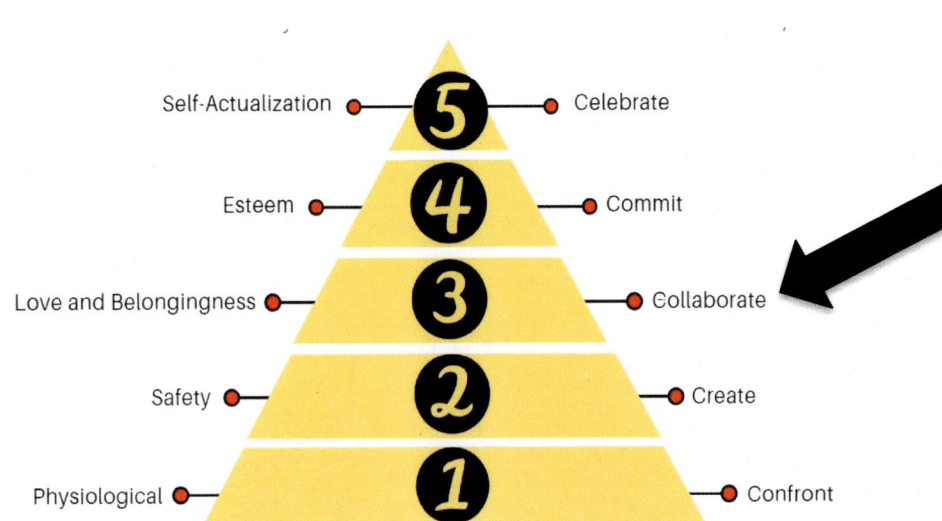

Self-Actualization ●	**5**	● Celebrate
Esteem ●	**4**	● Commit
Love and Belongingness ●	**3**	● Collaborate
Safety ●	**2**	● Create
Physiological ●	**1**	● Confront

Traffic Stop

Now that you have identified the story of your students, it should be clearer about who they are, their life-experiences, and their cultural values. ©ollaborate refers to a combined effort of sharing the story of your students through the curriculum, lessons, assignments, and practices. By actively practicing intentional inclusion, the educator **creates** a sense of belonging within their control – the classroom. Therefore, once you understand the students in your classroom, you will be willing to help your students to succeed. You will be motivated by their stories, helping them arrive to their destination safer, and you will be *endowed* with a portion of their *"why"*, as well as remembered for the role you played in helping them to realize it. You can only understand their *"why"*, once you have built trust and your students feel comfortable opening up to you. Now, this is your moment to begin to *apply* what you know about your students to the content, based on what you've learned as you *created* opportunities to get to know them better, as described in Chapter 2. This is your chance to help them ©ollaborate with you and others to make connections that foster a sense of belonging. In Maslow's Hierarchy of Needs, *"love and belonging"* is at the center *and* heart of it all. In our own life, we find a sense of connection with our family, friends, groups, organizations, profession, alumni, etc. Students need those *same* connections in the classroom, school, and community, and it's our job, as educators, to **create** that!

What we can control, is what we can control - our classroom. How do you ensure students feel a sense of community and belonging in your classroom? Do they feel included and valued for who they are? Peter Senge said, "All learners construct knowledge from an inner scaffolding of their individual and social experiences, emotions, will, aptitudes, beliefs, values, self-awareness, purpose, and more.

In other words, if you are learning in a classroom, **what** you understand is determined by **how** you understand things, **who** you are, and **what** you already know, as much as by **what** is covered, [as well as] **how** and **by whom** it is delivered."

Collaborating involves students becoming a part of the lessons, by being able to see some part of *their* story in the curriculum. The role of the educator is to incorporate students' stories into their subject-matter. The only way this task gets accomplished is if you excel at the traffic stop, "*Create*", by leveraging who the student is (culture, background, experiences, etc.), through collaborative efforts with you, the teacher. Students must collaborate with others to learn different perspectives from others' experiences. Our goal is to help model and prepare students for the world – painted with all the colors of the rainbow.

Application

- Enrich the curriculum with stories that reflect the demographics of your classroom. For example, in elementary classrooms, when teaching holiday traditions allow students to make personal connections with their family and/or cultural holiday traditions, and create time for them to share this with the class. Provide time for a class discussion that follows.

- Now that you are actively learning your students' stories, nurture their strengths through tasks in the classroom.

- Acknowledge and encourage student connection to your classroom and curriculum and when students bring their experiences to you, understand they trust you to use it for the good.

- Review your biases identified from Chapter One's *call* to confront. Create a plan to ensure you overcome those biases in an effort to not exclude anyone. The idea is to make the unconscious, <u>conscious</u>, to help change behaviors – helping ensure more students are being kept in, instead of pushed out, silenced, ignored, or assumed.

- Think about **collaborative** versus cooperative groups. Examine the differences to determine who is benefiting. Design lessons that shift the learning and allow students **collaborative** opportunities, rather than opportunities to simply cooperate with their peers. This will help students reach shared success, as they will all be considered as "contributors" to the learning and the accomplishments that derive from it. **Collaboration** takes intentional planning, and helps to transform student *compliance* with the learning, to students *partnering* with the learning, instead.

Reflection

1. What are positive ways to incorporate who your students are into your classroom? What are you intentionally doing to incorporate your students' various background?

2. Are your students' backgrounds considered, at all, in your classroom? If so, how does a student's background impact your classroom curriculum, lessons, assignments, and practices?

3. Do your students see *themselves* in your lessons? Stop and ask your students when was the last time they saw themselves in your lesson, classroom, content. Reflect on their response.

4. In what ways do you use collaboration as a tool to learn from each other? How do your students collaborate through activities to achieve a shared goal?

5. What are some ways to overcome challenges in collaboration where you may feel uncomfortable?

Curriculum tells their story!

In order to close the achievement gap, we give focus to our own story by addressing how our experiences shape our life. The next stop will examine ways to **commit** to *creating* a space that builds and

fosters meaningful relationships. Educators' **collaboration** of curriculum and culture, as well as their willingness and efficacy in partnering with their students to develop and implement this curriculum, will boost the confidence of their students, as well as

create an unwavering **commitment** to success!

Chapter 3 Notes: Collaborate

_____

_____

_____

_____

_____

_____

_____

_____

_____

_____

_____

_____

_____

_____

_____

_____

_____

_____

The Road to Equity

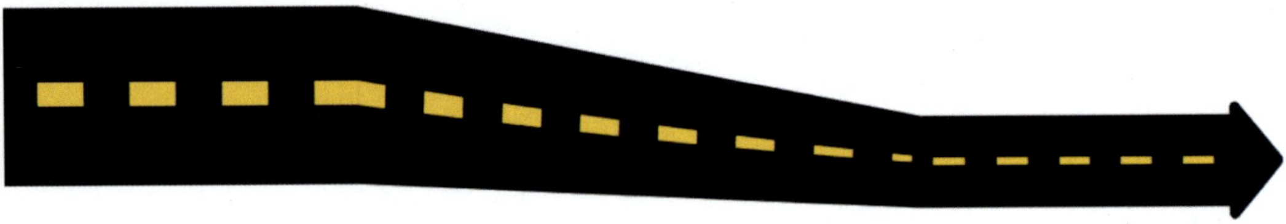

Chapter 4: **Commit**

*"Without involvement,
there is no commitment."*
Stephen Covey

I can recall each referral I wrote as a teacher because there were not too many, and because I was given no other alternative, after my attempts to deescalate a situation failed. On one occasion, when calling roll, I noticed one student, Marco, did not respond as his usual, enthusiastic self. I did not think much of it, as my brain was focused on the lesson for the day. When I attempted to start the class discussion, Marco refused to put away his phone, causing me to demand that he place it on my desk, temporarily, as his punishment. Even though he had been in my classroom for months and knew my expectations, rules, and procedures, he still refused. Despite the whispers of the other students, telling Marco to place the cell phone on my desk and reminding him that he would get it back at the end of class, if he did not make a big deal of it, Marco continued to be rebellious and belligerent. Unfortunately, after asking for his compliance numerous times and being blatantly denied and disobeyed, I felt I had no other choice but to write him up and phone home.

Upon calling home, I learned that Marco was having a tough time adjusting, while his mother was extremely sick, and his father was doing the best he could to keep everything together. It turned out, Marco was having a bad day, like many of us have. He did not need my challenging authority that day; he needed my grace. The next day, I asked Marco to speak with me, out in the hallway. I let him explain himself and his thoughts about what had happened, and I listened. I expressed my disappointment in his behavior, but understood his disposition and baggage he was carrying. It created a moment for me to extend my reach and make a **commitment** to him that I would not be judging him, based on a singular incident. I let him know that I was not going to follow through with the referral, and I made a commitment that from then on, my door and ear—for that matter— were open, accessible, and welcomed to him, and that I genuinely expected him to keep that in mind. Lastly, I reaffirmed that despite the situation, it was in the past, and he got a new, clean slate with me; deep down, I hoped that he would offer me the same...

Eye on Equity
Identify commitments
made by educator

_____

_____

_____

_____

_____

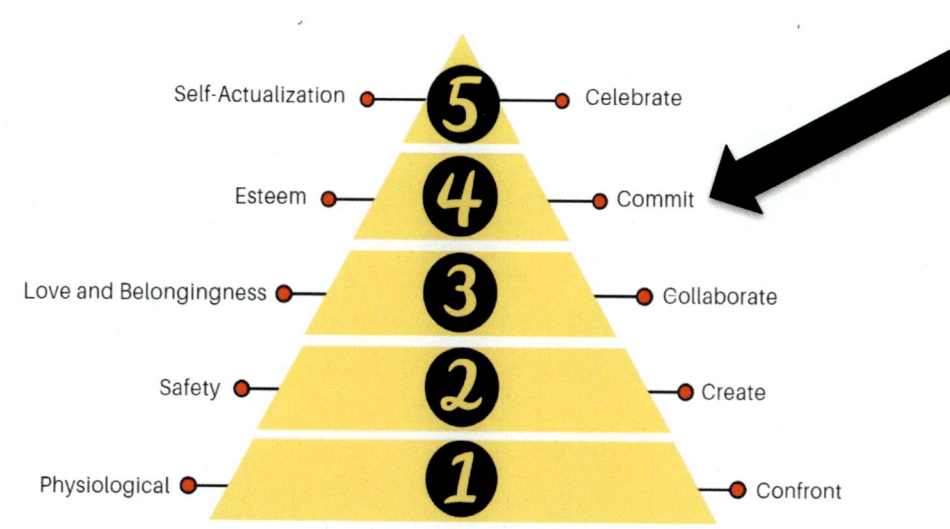

Traffic Stop

Commit refers to your outward expression of validating that what you said, is what you meant. **Commitment** is actionable, culturally-responsive communication and consistency that fosters esteem. When your students leave your classroom, how do they feel about themselves and their capabilities? Better yet, how do your students feel about themselves, *period*, following daily experiences in your classroom? Are you making deposits or withdrawals? A better question is this: Are you making *constructive* and *resonating* deposits into their lives, or are you *carelessly* making countless numbers of withdrawals, taking away from their self-esteem, hopes, and dreams? Because let's face it — every experience in life will either be a deposit or a withdrawal. Our experiences will either *add to or take away from*, and this is certainly true of the experiences that your students will have with you. Are certain students receiving more deposits than others? Who receives more withdrawals?

#WWSS: What would student's say?

In Maslow's hierarchy, before reaching self-actualization, a person develops their own **"sense of self: esteem, respect, and worth."** This *exit* that we must stop to take, on this "Road to Equity," discusses how your **commitment**, as the educator, is based on consistency to the previous pillars - confront, create, and collaborate. To systematically break the cycle, we must actively engage in **collaboration** and learning about our students to better serve them. Without a genuinely constructive **commitment**, your inconsistency is left up to the students' interpretation, and not only will they draw negative conclusions, but they will also doubt and question your intentions, further perpetuating the divide.

By making efforts that are seen by students, through your practices, policies, and communication, you are showing your students you value who they are, and, in turn, they will learn to value themselves. Building confidence within the confines of your classroom is necessary to create a "can-do" attitude for students in life and in your content area. When students feel valued for who they are and respected, they reciprocate and appreciate you because of your outward expression of consistency.

When we think back to our commitments, evaluate your biases and reflect on your **commitments** and **consistency**. Do your **commitments** extend to all students? Are you consistent? Be sure to refer back to your biases during this stop to review how they may unconsciously enter the classroom through subjective grading practices, privileges, and procedures. Communicating **commitment** happens in a variety of ways, creating a story all its own. It is expressed in the expectations you have for all students to succeed. Or do students consistently receive a message of low expectations from you? The environment, or your classroom, must be prepared for the audience you serve. How do you communicate diversity through your surroundings, and what message is it sending to your students? It is not just with our words that we communicate how we feel towards students and even adults for that matter, but with non-verbal cues, power, décor, curriculum, attitude, expectations, standards, perceptions, and more.

A dear friend and principal, Jenise Wright, said, "Words have the power to hurt, help, or heal; ALWAYS choose the latter two." Communication means having challenging conversations to bring about change and models for students' voices to be heard and their student culture to be embraced. To add to this, sometimes what people do *not* say is an answer in and of itself. Remember, as a child, I felt what many of my teachers said, without them saying it, at all. Not only do words have power, but all of our interactions have the power to hurt, help, or heal our students.

Building a culture takes **commitment**, and change starts with one person. **You** have the power to **commit** to equity and transform your classroom. And think, if everyone is viewing education with an eye towards equity, your campus and ultimately your community would develop unity built on justice, fairness, and respect. The climate of your classroom will tell its own story, reflective of your leadership's vision of respect, high expectations for all learners, and what is valued.

Consider the following chart as reflective of the differences encompassed by a large portion of your students or areas that have influence over how a student may see the world.

Now, take a moment to examine and reflect on ways to be more inclusive with conscious thought towards your principles, practices, and concepts. What tone do these set for the climate of your classroom? Your visual classroom is sometimes your first impression for a student, and it is the outward expression of your commitment that they'll see and feel, first, shaping their own judgments about their school year with you. As the educator, set the climate and tone of your classroom by consciously making efforts to showcase your **commitment** to your students' learning, keeping in mind that your students should be at the heart of all that you do in your classroom, in order to maximize their learning potential.

Factors to consider when preparing your classroom:

- ✓ Accessibility
- ✓ Gender-neutral
- ✓ Class Décor (colors, lighting, posters, bulletin boards)
- ✓ Culturally-Conscious: Diversity & Representation
- ✓ Communication: Verbal & Non-Verbal

REAL-WORLD REPRESENTATION

*"I tend to look at art and drawings especially in elementary. I am looking for representation. Although, what is available is majority white – this not reflective of **all** my students. I include in all poster's equal amounts of different students, reflective of our classroom and the world. Posters to include disability, group pictures where everyone feels included, girls doing math and science, non-traditional career and gender roles, etc."*

–Joanna Hicks, Elementary Teacher

Application

- Be purposeful and intentional with your classroom designs. A great resource is *Shouting Won't Grow Dendrites: 20 Techniques to Detour around the Danger Zones,* by Marcia L. Tate, who outlines research-based best practices for creating a physical environment conducive to learning.
    - Color: (i.e., Certain colors excite and energize; others calm and relax)
    - Lighting: Natural light is best, if possible
    - Displays: Representative of your students, depicting and showing your **commitment** and belief in their success

- Build confidence in your students within your classroom by starting with ice-breakers, team-building, and low-level introductory or prior knowledge skills to create the mindset of "I can."

- Practice giving your students positive, non-academic compliments to begin making deposits into your students.

- **Commit** to your students' education by showing them that you care. Make the effort to contact their parent/guardian regularly (either through weekly mass or individual emails and/or individual phone calls), and ALWAYS begin your communication with positives!

- Let students know you care about them, beyond the classroom. This lets them know you see them as a person. Comment or highlight student engagement in activities, on and off the campus, letting students know that there is so much more to them beyond what you see in your classroom. We only hope our students give us this same grace when we extend it to them. (This is also a great classroom management tool.)

Reflection

1. How do you communicate your commitment to your students?

2. What does consistency look like from a student's perspective? Have you been consistent with your commitments to your students?

3. Do your students feel valued for who they are? How do you instill confidence in *all* your students?

4. Does the environment reflect your commitment to the learner(s)?

5. What story would your classroom tell from observation alone?

Climate tells a story!

Commitment derives from the culture and climate you have prepared for your students. Educators must be intentional in practices, through applied effort. On this route, the educator's goal is defined as "actions aligning with their beliefs." In the next chapter, you will examine the final stop, *celebration*, and its role on the "Road to Equity."

Chapter 4 Notes: Commit

Chapter 5: *Celebrate*

"An individual has not started living until he can rise above the narrow confines of his individualistic concerns to the broader concerns of all humanity."
Dr. Martin Luther King, Jr.

Coming from a predominately white high school, *ironically*, I was nervous about entering the classroom, as a first-year teacher, at a school where students looked like me. I know this may come as a surprise, but if you have learned a little bit about me during this journey, you know my past shaped my outlook. It was a culture shock, to say the least, entering a classroom to teach a class filled with *black* students who looked like me, and I was fully aware of how my nervousness might have consciously or unconsciously spilled into my classroom management. Nevertheless, I did not cower my expectations because of my feelings, rather, I boldly set the expectations of firm, fair, and fun.

Upon learning about my students, I did not expect collaborative groups to work together peacefully, exchanging ideas and even disagreeing respectfully (*most* of the time). Yet, day in and day out, I observed a mixture of kids who reflected all the colors of America – sitting in my classroom with all their differences – and working to-gether with no issues. When *one* person celebrated, we *all* did. We were learning together, laughing, and talking about tough stuff too.

We were bonding and bridging pathways that translated into the feeling of "I see you."

As a student, I knew what it felt like to not be seen, but instead, assumed and devalued. I vowed to ensure my students felt comfortable in their skin for who they were and understood that each was a valuable, contributing member to our learning. We became a family, *celebrating* through the **confrontation** of my *own* biases, *creating* opportunities to connect, collaborating with the curriculum, and **committing** to the work. More importantly, I created a space for my students to work with others who did not look like them, modeled it, *and* made it safe.

Eye on Equity:
Why is it important
to celebrate differences?

_____

_____

_____

_____

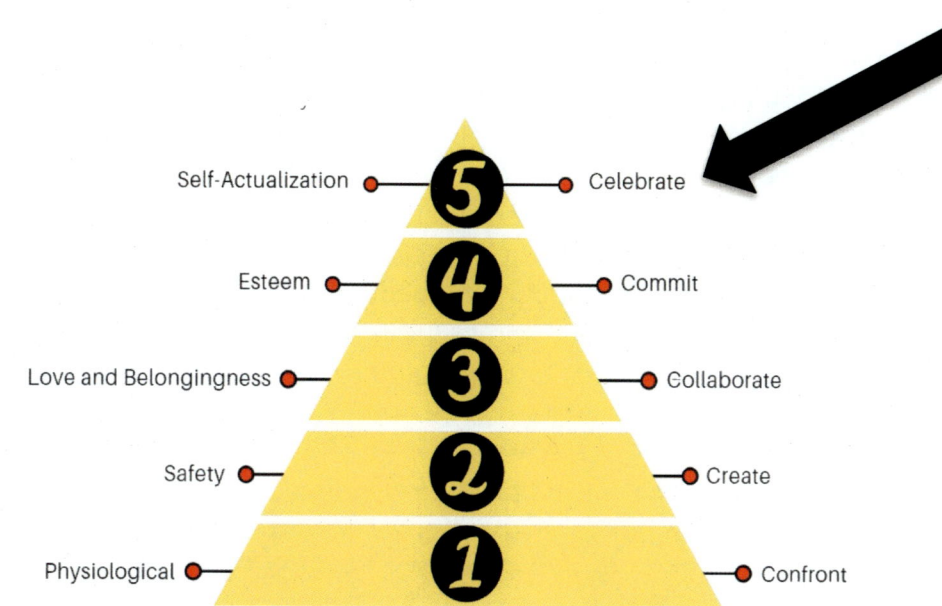

Traffic Stop

Celebrate refers to the ability and willingness to be **open-minded towards those who are different from you, by embracing who they are and praising it**. Celebration is your willingness, as an educator, to bravely help students find their voice in their own story and helping them to be confident in who they are and their abilities. What role does your classroom, or you for that matter, play in shaping your students? Embracing differences comes in all shapes, sizes, amounts, and colors. These differences include race, socio-economic status, national origin, sexual orientation, religion, disability, immigration status, English Language Learners (ELLs), low-income, LGBTQ+ (lesbian, gay, bisexual, transgender, queer, and any other all-encompassing expression of gender identity and/or sexual orientation), occupation, location, etc. When we embrace diversity, we learn from each other. It provides a mechanism to dispel stereotypes and creates a new narrative.

Why is diversity important? I embrace diversity because it is the right thing to do. It's the right thing to do because everybody is different, whether physically, spiritually, financially, geographically, etc., and to frown upon others because they are different from you is just *wrong* and simply a very wasteful and meaningless use of energy and time. So, again, as educators we must embrace diversity and model this for our students. We must prepare them for the world that we wish to see because they have seen it—in our classrooms and they modeled it through our leadership. Your students will know they are valued, *celebrated*, and above all, loved. This is being authentic, understanding, empathetic, and granting people grace because we have all needed a little of each at one time or another.

(Refer to **Appendix C**) In addition, our "Equitable Classroom Checklist" is available is with our Train-The-Trainer program.

As a person masters each level in Maslow's Hierarchy of Needs and develops positive self-esteem, a person can **reach their full actualized self or potential**. People are shaped by every other level below them and motivated, now, by justice, wisdom, meaning, critical-thinking, and purpose. To construct a more equitable classroom, by reaching the highest point, means you, as the educator, have made a concerted and combined effort to embrace the differences within your classroom, identify biases within yourself, and navigate connections by communicating and collaborating, in spite of all the barriers.

Celebration comes in many forms. The most important tool at the disposal of an educator is the power of feedback and praise. In, *Assessment for Learning: Putting It into Practice*, the authors state, "Feedback that focuses on what needs to be done can encourage all to believe that they can improve." Utilize feedback as an opportunity to help students grow and build confidence in their capabilities and potential as learners. We can use feedback as a tool to help students grow and become confident in their skills and talents. We should never use feedback as an *assault* on who they are, chipping away at (and withdrawing from) their sense of self. If you have built a meaningful relationship on commitment and consistency, you will be able to provide feedback out of love and no other reason.

I connected with being a student and remembering the lack of praise and acknowledgement from my own teachers made me a lot more *intentional* in my efforts to give my students frequent praise and positive feedback. I thought back to only a single teacher from elementary, Ms. Greene, who built up my confidence with words of praise. I remembered my own words of affirmation that I delivered as a teacher and even as an administrator. Again, words have power.

Praise tells the student, "*I* see you." Choosing praise over punishment translates to **so much more. To some students, praise translates into...**

- Acknowledgment of "me", individually, as a student, verbalized with positive words because it is something I do not hear at home - often or at all (or I only hear feedback when I mess up, so I'm afraid to try in your class for fear of messing up and getting the same result...).

- Praise helps teachers to "see" and acknowledge students who they may not connect with on the surface (i.e. race, socio-economic, disability, life experiences, etc.). It translates to action from students: "YOU are safe to take risks, when you are in my classroom, without fear of receiving solely negative feedback, but the understanding that our relationship is built on both—positive and structured feedback—for growth."

- For some, it means "you," the teacher (an adult) – see "me," (a student) in a world that I feel does not see me *at all*.

- For some, praise from a teacher who does not look like the student, may be the *first* positive feedback the student has received by a teacher who does not share the same background. (Think back to my experience with Ms. Greene.) Therefore, use praise as an opportunity to shift the mindset of a student who may have consistently heard negative feedback from other teachers who may share your *same* background. (For example, a white student thinking all black teachers are... [Fill in the blank] and vice versa.)

- For some, praise translates into little *milestone* **celebrations**. As the educator, making deposits into students is essential, because we know that ultimately, they will slip up (they are kids, after all, and learning is a messy process.). Nevertheless, the more deposits that are made of the positives, the more the positives will overshadow some of the unavoidable negatives or withdrawals that might be made. Therefore, when the educator *does* have to express disapproval of any student's behavior, the feedback does not drop the student into a place of negativity and a feeling of defeat, as there is a shared understanding, now, due to the consistency of praise, that we have established a relationship, and that the disapproval is coming from a place of love and care.

By choosing praise over punishment, educators see positive results. Challenge yourself to NOT look at praise as simply words or feedback, but as an opportunity to foster meaningful relationships built on love.

Paul Gorski said, "We cannot *'Multicultural Arts Fair'* our way to racial justice in schools." Paul is right. It takes more than an *event* to truly **celebrate** the gift each student has to offer the world. Your job, as the educator, is to help to let it shine, not to dim it. You do this by **celebrating** students for their treasures, their progress, their growth, and their kindness. You begin to **celebrate** them for who they are and what they bring to the table, instead of your own expectations or the world's. When you arrive at the **celebration** destination, your classroom exhibits inclusivity, respects differences, and utilizes the strength of each student, symbolizing the classroom unit as a *family*, all striving to reach the same destination – success. By understanding the barriers faced by your students and how their experiences shape their world, we can utilize their experiences to lift their voice, by nurturing their strengths with acknowledgement, feedback, and covered with love. All the previous stories give way to the story of your classroom as a whole. Would differences be celebrated or ignored? Would students feel comfortable to express their views without risks? Again (as asked in the previous chapter), what story would your classroom tell by observation?

Application

- Showcase positive examples and interaction of all cultures (overcoming the generally negative stereotypes to break the cycle).

- *Create* meaningful lessons that illicit opportunities for students to learn, research, and **discover** success in your content, through people who are similar to them, as well as different to ensure balance.

- Develop a "Cultural-Conscious Committee", on your campus, meeting monthly to *celebrate* your school's diversity. Focus on promoting monthly targets and reminders to faculty and students (i.e. bulletin boards, monthly, planned focuses that the whole school can push, exemplary work, etc.), to serve as the model of equitable practices. Be a model of equitable practices and an equitable leader.

- *Celebrate* non-academic successes, such as character traits in students, recognizing the strengths of the whole child.

- Establish positive relationships through praise and feedback (foundational), before *ever* criticizing.

Reflection

1. Do your classroom policies and practices *celebrate* differences and highlight the strengths of your students?

2. In what ways, do you use the differences within your classroom as a tool for learning, respectively *and* appropriately?

3. How can you model the "*celebration* of differences" for your students?

4. What current praise and feedback techniques do you use? How can you use these two techniques, praise and feedback, equitably and to embrace diversity and inclusion?

5. Looking through a lens of equity, what story would your class-room, now, tell and reveal about you, your students, your curriculum, your climate, and the classroom experiences that you *create*? You have the power, as the educator, to control the narrative, perpetuate the narrative, or change the narrative. If you do not create the story of your classroom, students will create their own without your input.

Your Classroom tells a story!

Congratulations! By embarking on *The Road to Equity,* you have made the first commitment to being a Barrier-Breaker for your students! By utilizing the best practices to reach a more equitable classroom, **all** students will benefit and the gap will begin to narrow. By embracing our differences, we can help more students on the path to success, access to resources, and opportunities to change the narrative. I always remind myself, what we do with our life is our gift to the world, a part of our gift, as educators, is to help students discover their gift, celebrate who they are, and empower students to write and share their story, helping to do *their* part to change the world.

Chapter 5 Notes: Celebrate

"When a flower doesn't bloom,
you fix the environment in which it
grows, not the flower."
Alexander Den Heijer

Appendix A

- "Project Implicit" Implicit Association Test

  https://implicit.harvard.edu/implicit/takeatest.html

List your results...

✔ _____

✔ _____

✔ _____

✔ _____

✔ _____

Think about how your biases impact your classroom, line by line, based on your results.

✓ _____

✓ _____

✓ _____

✓ _____

✓ _____

What actionable steps can you take to move towards equity to overcome your biases, now that you are aware?

✓ _____

✓ _____

✓ _____

✓ _____

✓ _____

Set a goal. Make it happen.

Next steps on #TheRoadToEquity

My Accountability Partner

Appendix B: Cultural Iceberg

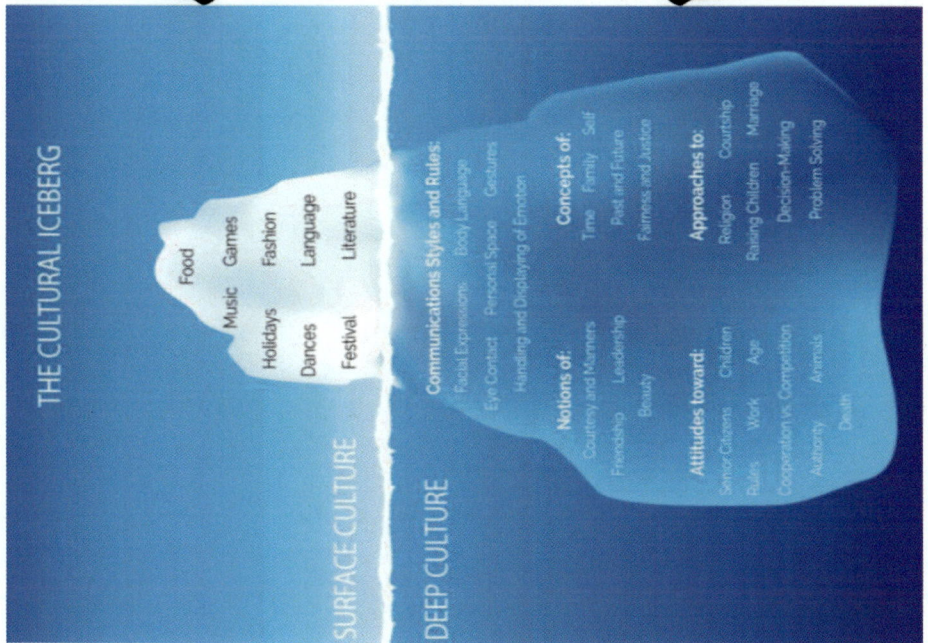

The Five C's To Construct an Equitable Classroom

MK Results, LLC.
The Road to Equity

Equity is giving each student what they need to be successful.

Sounds like
1. Acknowledgement of student responses and input
2. Challenging the status quo & failure
3. Clear defined guidance and expectations for what it takes to succeed
4. Involvement and respectful communication to all stakeholders
5. Everyone's story heard and represented
6. Friendly and courageous conversations
7. Active listening, feedback, praise, and probing
8. Not reinforcing stereotypes and dismantling barriers
9. An invitation to be included in the process
10. Assumption of positive intentions

Feels like
1. Climate is safe and welcoming for all students
2. Positive culture of firm and fair
3. Accessible to learning, the teacher, resources, and enrichment
4. Cares about the learning of each student
5. Lessons, procedures, and polices are inclusive initiatives
6. Multiple perspectives are represented
7. High expectations for all students
8. Community of learners through relationship building
9. Peer support encouraged
10. Collaborative versus Cooperative

Looks Like
1. Identifying prior knowledge and interaction through conversation
2. Greetings students by name
3. Eye-contact & proximity for all learners (non-verbal cues)
4. Inclusive of school, parent, community partnership
5. Story of your students reflected in visual aids
6. Respectful relationships between T/S, S/T, S/S
7. Clear expectations, rules, and procedures outlined
8. Variety of teaching strategies to support all learners
9. Relevant and current events to make connections
10. Leading by example

THE ROAD TO EQUITY

MK Results, LLC.
The Road to Equity

The 5 C's To Construct an Equitable Classroom

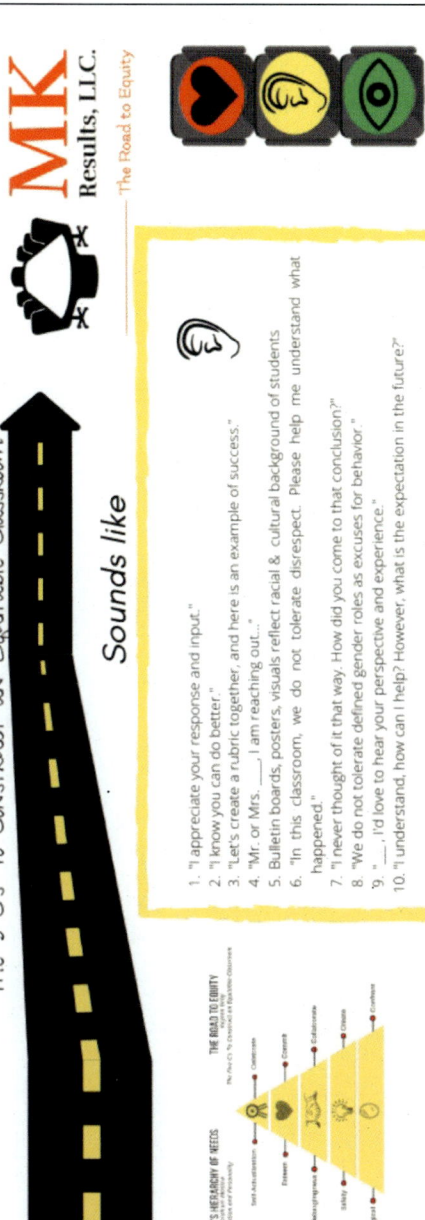

MASLOW'S HIERARCHY OF NEEDS

THE ROAD TO EQUITY

Sounds like

1. "I appreciate your response and input."
2. "I know you can do better."
3. "Let's create a rubric together, and here is an example of success."
4. "Mr. or Mrs.____ I am reaching out..."
5. Bulletin boards, posters, visuals reflect racial & cultural background of students
6. "In this classroom, we do not tolerate disrespect. Please help me understand what happened."
7. "I never thought of it that way. How did you come to that conclusion?"
8. "We do not tolerate defined gender roles as excuses for behavior."
9. "____, I'd love to hear your perspective and experience."
10. "I understand, how can I help? However, what is the expectation in the future?"

Feels like

1. Be who you are. Vulnerability is a feeling.
2. Because I love you enough, I am addressing this with you. It does not mean I love you less; I am disappointed in your choices.
3. I am available to all students and our bi-weekly temperature checks help determine academically and emotionally where students are by simply asking, "Is there anything you need from me?"
4. "Are you okay? How can I help you? Do you need to talk? Do you need a minute?"
5. I never knew there was a black female mathematician who made phenomenal discoveries in space exploration.
6. You bring different perspectives for the students to evaluate and think critically, not just one or the majority opinion.
7. Do not accept mediocre for some students and not challenge others on the basis of your biases.
8. What are your cultural traditions, values, and customs?
9. Students learning from others' experiences, creating empathy
10. If our class is a community, what are we working towards and how will we all ensure we get there...together?

Looks Like

1. "How has your own experience related to this story?"
2. "Good afternoon, Kayren! It's a good day!"
3. Set the tone for the power zone.
4. Communication defined and expectations of all stakeholders
5. Positive images, posters, and celebrations reflective of your student demographics - messages of reflective success
6. Are students quiet when you are talking and while others are talking?
7. Collaborative expectations visual in classroom, communicated, defined, and given examples
8. Differentiation and teaching strategies to support a variety of learning styles
9. "What are some sacrifices, challenges, or obstacles you have had to overcome?"
10. Setting the example through your interactions with students who are different, models to others students what respect looks like.

Appendix D: The Five C's

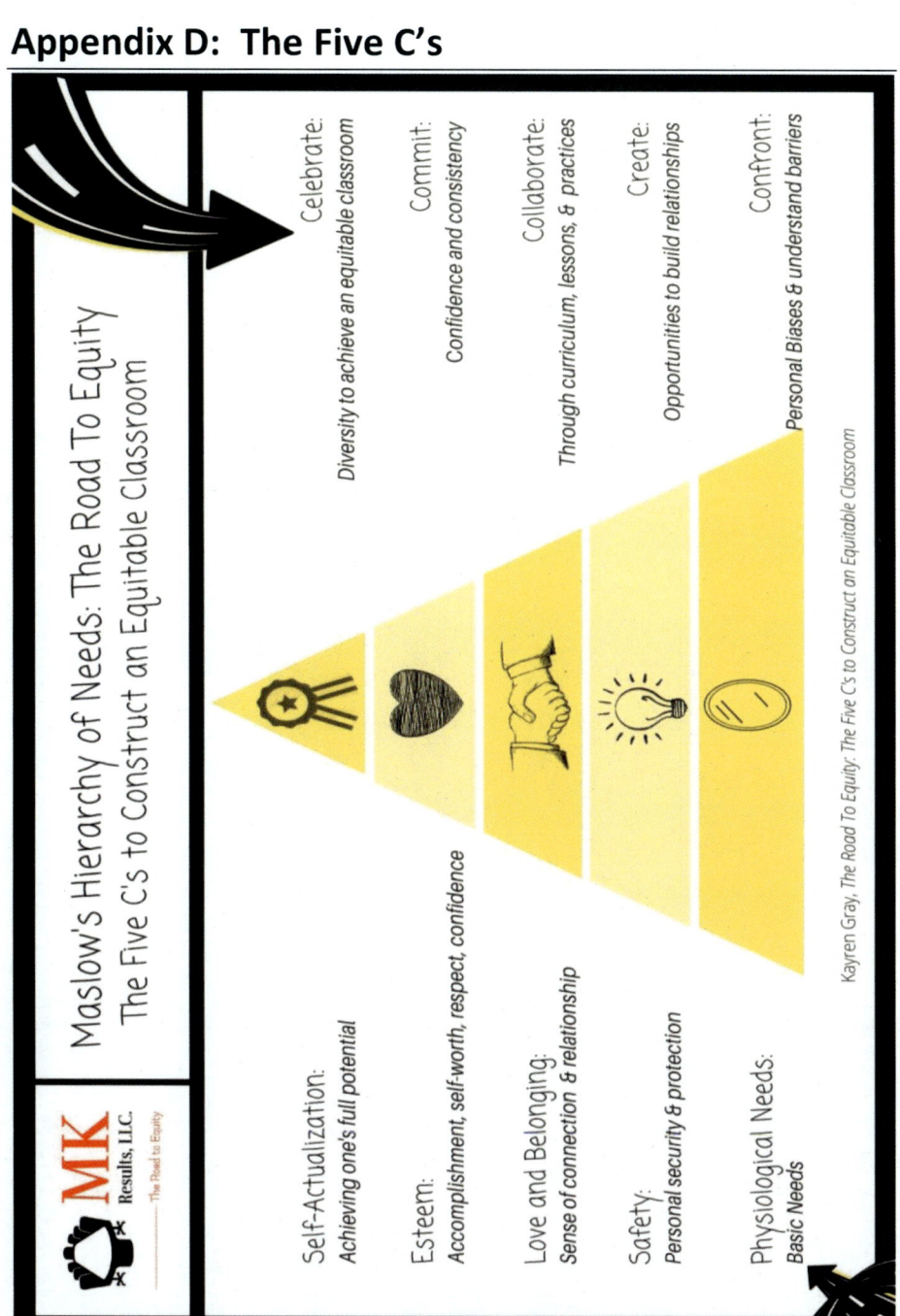

Maslow's Hierarchy of Needs: The Road To Equity
The Five C's to Construct an Equitable Classroom

MK Results, LLC. — The Road to Equity

Celebrate:
Diversity to achieve an equitable classroom

Commit:
Confidence and consistency

Collaborate:
Through curriculum, lessons, & practices

Create:
Opportunities to build relationships

Confront:
Personal Biases & understand barriers

Self-Actualization:
Achieving one's full potential

Esteem:
Accomplishment, self-worth, respect, confidence

Love and Belonging:
Sense of connection & relationship

Safety:
Personal security & protection

Physiological Needs:
Basic Needs

Kayren Gray, *The Road To Equity: The Five C's to Construct an Equitable Classroom*

Appendix E: Texas Equitable Roadmap

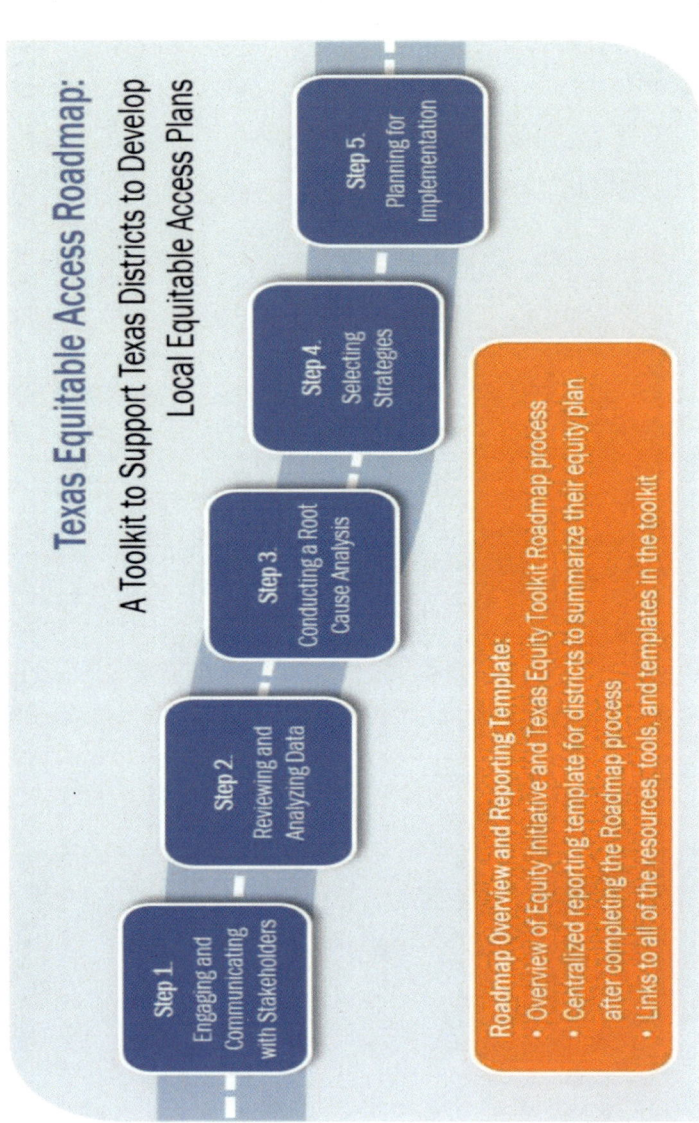

Texas Equitable Access Roadmap:
A Toolkit to Support Texas Districts to Develop Local Equitable Access Plans

Step 1.
Engaging and Communicating with Stakeholders

Step 2.
Reviewing and Analyzing Data

Step 3
Conducting a Root Cause Analysis

Step 4.
Selecting Strategies

Step 5.
Planning for Implementation

Roadmap Overview and Reporting Template:
- Overview of Equity Initiative and Texas Equity Toolkit Roadmap process
- Centralized reporting template for districts to summarize their equity plan after completing the Roadmap process
- Links to all of the resources, tools, and templates in the toolkit

[1] For more information on the Every Student Succeeds Act, visit http://www.ed.gov/essa?src=rn. Information on equity as it relates to states is included in section (1111(g)(1)(B)). Information on equity as it relates to districts is included in section (1112(b)(2)).

Appendix F: Tell Your Story

Jot down your story and what you want your students to know about you. How can your story connect to your students? Doodle it, write it out, and reflect!

Appendix G: Closing the Gap

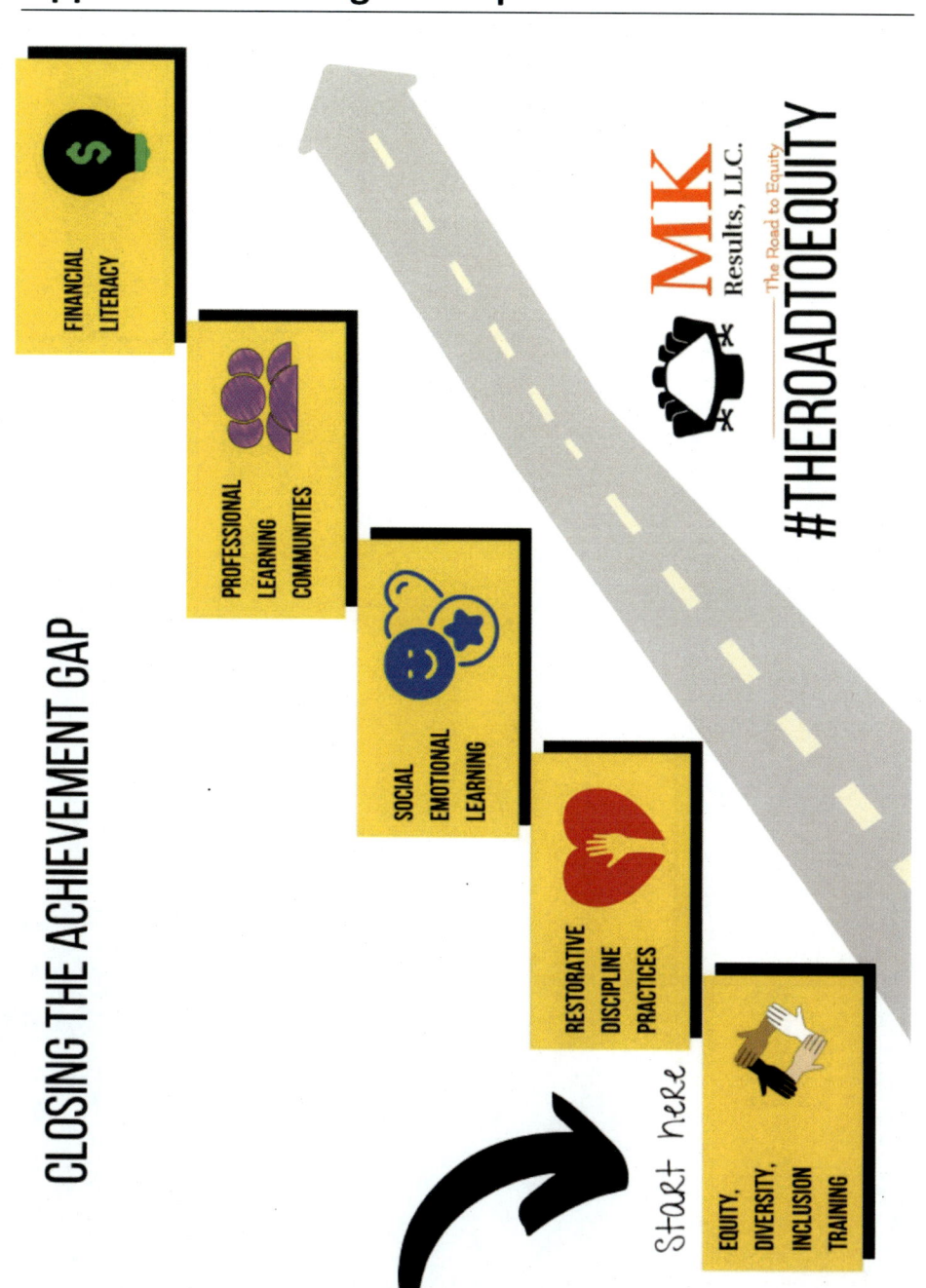

Appendix H: The Road to Equity

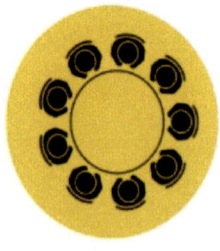

Equality

- Equal access to opportunities
- Treating everyone the same

Diversity

- Everyone is different
- Diversity in people, perspectives, and positions

Inclusion

- Sense of belonging
- Response to the needs of ALL students
- ALL voices/experiences/ stories represented
- ALL *feel* heard & included

Equity

- Process to reach equality
- Fair, inclusive, access to education and opportunities to multiple pathways to reach success
- Reflective in policy, practices, procedures

Asks:

Who is at the table?

Has everyone been heard?

Who is trying to sit at the table but can't? What barriers and roadblocks are preventing and prohibiting?

MK Results, LLC.
The Road to Equity

www.mkresultsllc.com

Appendix I: Why Equity?

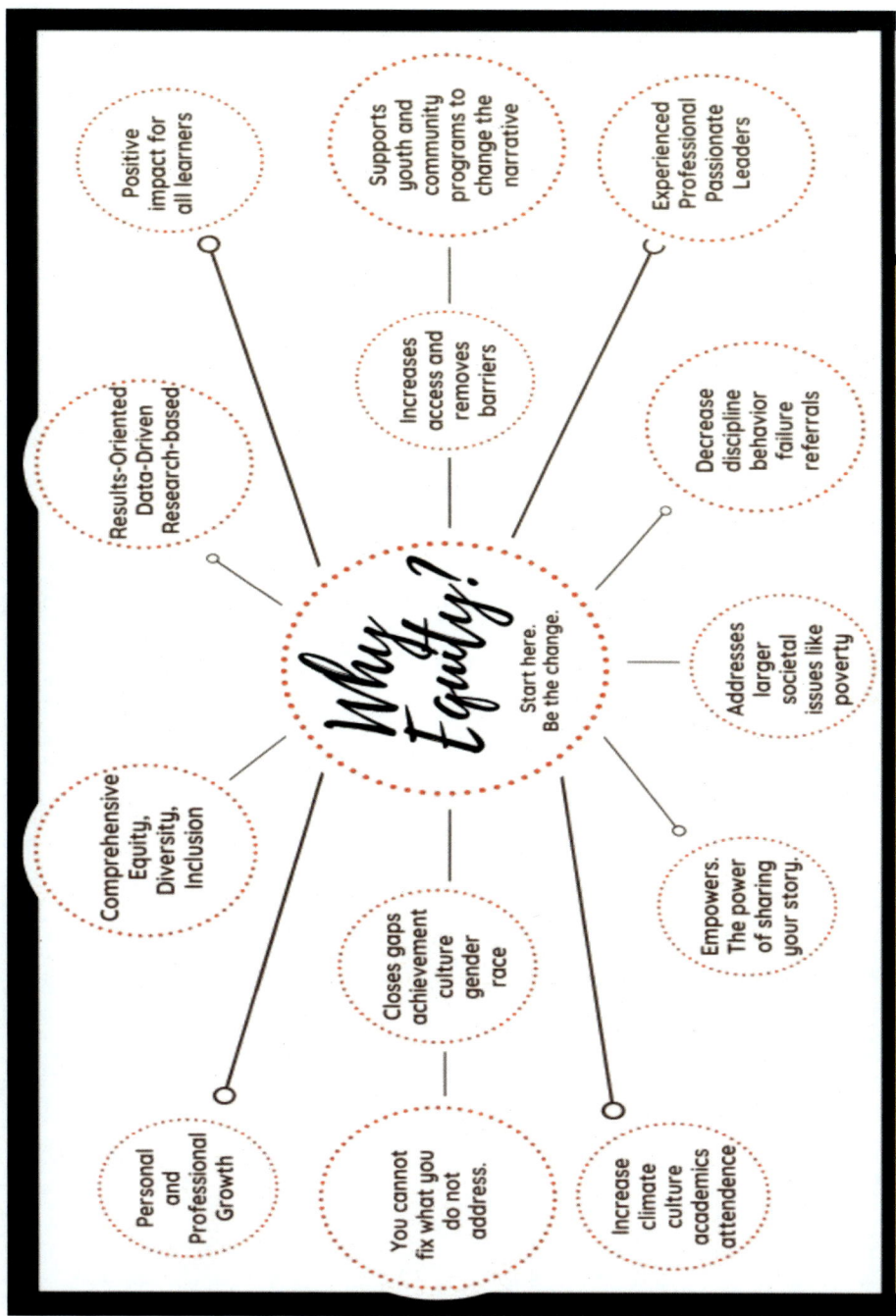

References

Aud, S., Wilkinson-Flicker, S., Kristapovich, P., Rathbun, A., Wang, X., & Zhang, J. (2013). *The condition of education.*

Au, K. (2009). *Isn't culturally responsive instruction just good teaching?* Social Education. 73(4), 179-183.

Blanchard, Carlos, & Randolph. (2001). *Empowerment Takes More than A Minute* p. 32.

Bennett, M., Barrett, M., Karakozov, R., Kipiani, G., Lyons, E., Pavlenko, V., & Riazanova., T. (2004). *Young children's evaluations of the ingroup and of out groups: A multi-national study.* Social Development, 13(1), 124–141.

Black, Harrison, Lee, et al. (2005). *Assessment for Learning: Putting It into Practice.*

Conchas, G. Q., & Noguera, P. A. (2004). Understanding the exceptions: How small schools support the achievement of academically successful Black boys. In N. Way & J. Y. Chu (Eds.*), Adolescent boys: Exploring diverse cultures of boyhood* (pp. 317– 337). New York, NY: New York University Press.

Cummins, J. (2007). *Pedagogies for the poor? Realigning reading instruction for low-income students with scientifically based reading research.* Educational Researcher, 36(9), 564–572.

DuFour, DuFour, and Eaker.(2002). *Getting Started: Reculturing Schools to Become Professional Learning Communities.*

Fisher, Frey, & Hattie. (2018). *Developing Assessment-Capable Visible Learners, Grades K- 12.*

Gay, G. (2010). *Culturally responsive teaching: Theory, research, and practice* (2nd ed.). New York, NY: Teachers College Press.

Harry, B., & Klingner, J. K. (2006). *Why are so many minority students in special education? Understanding race and disability in schools.* New York, NY: Teachers College Press.

Krasnoff, Basha (2016). *Culturally Responsive Teaching: A Guide to Evidence-Based Practices for Teaching All Students Equitably*. Region X Equity Assistance Center Education Northwest.

Ladson-Billings, G. (2009). *The Dreamkeepers: Successful teachers of African American children* (2nd ed.). San Francisco, CA: Jossey-Bass.

Orosco, M. J. (2010). *A sociocultural examination of Response to Intervention with Latino English language learners.* Theory Into Practice, 49(4), 265–272

Orosco, M. J., & Klingner, J. (2010). *One school's implementation of RTI with English language learners*: "Referring into RTI". Journal of Learning Disabilities, 43(3), 269–288

Orosco, M. J., & O'Connor, R. E. (2011). Cultural aspects of teaching reading with Latino English language learners.

Muhammad, Anthony. (2015). Overcoming the achievement gap trap: Liberating mindsets to effect change. Solution Tree.

Payne, Ruby. (2008). *Under Resourced Learners: 8 Strategies to Boost Student Achievement.*

Sanders, M. G. (Ed.). (2000). *Schooling students placed at risk: Research, policy, and practice in the education of poor and minority adolescents.* Mahwah, NJ: Lawrence Erlbaum.

Scott, B. (2000). *We should not kid ourselves: Excellence requires equity.* IDRA Newsletter, 27(2), 1–2, 8–10.

Tate, M. L. (2007). Shouting won't grow dendrites: 20 techniques for managing a brain-compatible classroom. Corwin Press.

Webography

https://www.avid.org/equity

https://www.edglossary.org/

https://nces.ed.gov/fastfacts/display.asp?id=805

https://www.pacer.org/bullying/resources/stats.asp

https://www.edweek.org/ew/issues/education-statistics/index.html

https://www2.ed.gov/about/offices/list/ocr/docs/2013-14-first-look.pdf

https://ocrdata.ed.gov/Downloads/CRDC-School-Discipline-Snapshot.pdf

Glossary

Bias: prejudice in favor or against one thing, person, or group

Explicit Bias: Conscious attitudes of qualities to a certain group; result of a perceived threat

Implicit Bias: Unconscious attitudes of qualities to a certain group shaped by your experience and learned associations

Collaborative effort: the action exerted by the educator to infuse the story of their students into the story of their classroom (i.e. curriculum, procedures, policies, etc.)

Equity: refers to promoting fairness through actions, policies, hiring, and resources (especially in education) to facilitate practices that are attainable for all; giving each individual what is needed and/or fair chance.

Equitable Leader: refers to a someone who is willing to hold others accountable; someone who is positive and displays a growth mindset striving to put forth the intentional practices of equity in their daily life.

Diversity: refers to embracing differences with respect; refers to equitable representation that embraces inclusivity, especially in leadership; variety.

Inclusion: the act of including students in innovative ways to your classroom and school for that matter to ensure they are involved and a contributing member to the classroom based on their ability

Culture: refers to collective traits (customs, arts, social institutions, expression, achievements, etc.) that define a particular group; utilized as an asset and resource to understand one another's differences. (Explore how culture has and can evolve over time).

Holistic Approach: refers to a "whole-person" approach and factors that are necessary to create a more equitable society (i.e. thinking about the big picture; more than curriculum)

Perception: the ability to become more aware of different lens that shape how people see the world and learn.

Prejudice: unfavorable bias, dislike, unjust behavior from unfounded opinions.

Racism: the belief and use of race as a means to distinguish your race as superior to others

Self-Awareness: refers to the element of being "self-woke" about your bias, prejudices, and experiences and how they shape the world around you.

Socio-economic status: refers to the income, status, education, and even career choice used to measure the level of respect for reciprocated

Stereotype: a fixed and oversimplified view of a group of people

Temperature Tuesday: This is a way to gauge the temperature of your classroom and your students by intentionally setting aside a day to check-in with each of your students. You can do this during a time where students are working and call them over to you to have a conversation. Visit our website for resources and questions to ask during this mini-conference focused on academics, social emotional, life, circumstances, and more with your students.

Author, leader, educator, administrator, parent, advocate, speaker, and consultant, Kayren has dedicated her life to closing the gap and ensuring student success. On her classroom board read, "The quality of your life depends on the choices you make" pushing her students to be the writers of their own story and utilizing education as the key. She champions for *all* students to succeed by empowering students, but especially educators, to change the narrative – one person at a time.

Kayren earned her Bachelor's Degree in Political Science from Texas A&M Central Texas and Master's Degree from Lamar University in Educational Administration with Principal Certification. Entering public education nearly a decade ago, her focus was to share her own passion for learning with others and ultimately, impact the lives of students who felt that history—or school for that matter—was not for them. She soon realized and began to understand how important it is for students of color to see success in people who look like them. By building meaningful relationships and making learning culturally-relevant, Mrs. Gray vowed to equip students with not just content, but skills they can utilize beyond school and in the real world. In 2014, she was recognized as Ellison High School's Teacher of the Year and Killeen ISD Secondary Teacher of the Year Finalist. As an administrator, she focused on the climate and culture and the correlation between student-engagement and academic achievement. Despite various roles in education, Kayren has continuously asked the same question, "Is this the best decision for all students?"

Kayren Gray is the author of *The Road to Equity: The Five C's to Construct an Equitable Classroom* and founder of MK Results, LLC. formed from a collective team of like-minded educators with a vision to change the narrative, empower others, and be examples of embracing diversity. Our platform was founded to facilitate a conversation on equity and to share a powerful message on the impact of unity, diversity, inclusion, and cultural competency.

Kayren is a military spouse with one son and two bonus sons. She resides in Harker Heights, Texas where she is active in the community and enjoys traveling. Her personal and professional experience has afforded her the honor to share her experiences to transform leaders and organizations on their path to peak performance focusing representing the varied human experience by having and creating a seat at the table. In her pastime, Kayren hosts weekly podcast entitled, "The Road to Equity" and the "Educators' Round-Table." Finally finding her own voice, she hopes to continue to share and embark on a journey towards growth and understanding through 'A Friendly Conversation.'

Be a Barrier Breaker

Visit our website for more resources, programs, and training related to this title and more.

Download the eBook available on Amazon or listen on Audible.

Join in on the conversation by connecting:

 https://www.facebook.com/mkresultsllc

https://www.facebook.com/groups/beabarrierbreaker

 www.linkedin.com/in/kayrengraymkresults

 Search: MKRESULTSLLC

 Listen to our weekly podcast available on all platforms.

Search: The Road to Equity

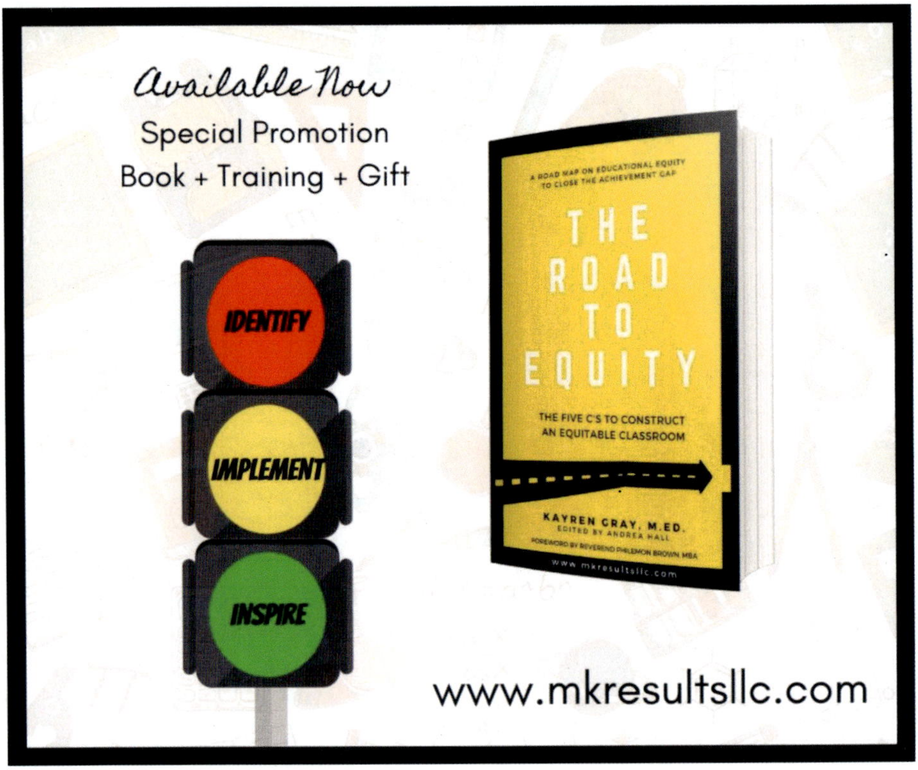

Workshops | Training | Seminars

www.mkresultsllc.com

The Road to Equity

The Five C's to Construct an Equitable Classroom

Essential Questions:

1. Are you looking for a culturally-relevant learning experience for your students?

2. Are you seeking professional development focused on equity, diversity, and inclusion practices?

3. Are you seeking best practices to serve ALL students on their individual path to success?

4. Are you concerned about any achievement gaps in your classroom, campus, or district?

Online Virtual Training Options Available

Be a Barrier Breaker

Contact us today to reserve your spot to

#close the gap on #theroadtoequity

Coming Soon

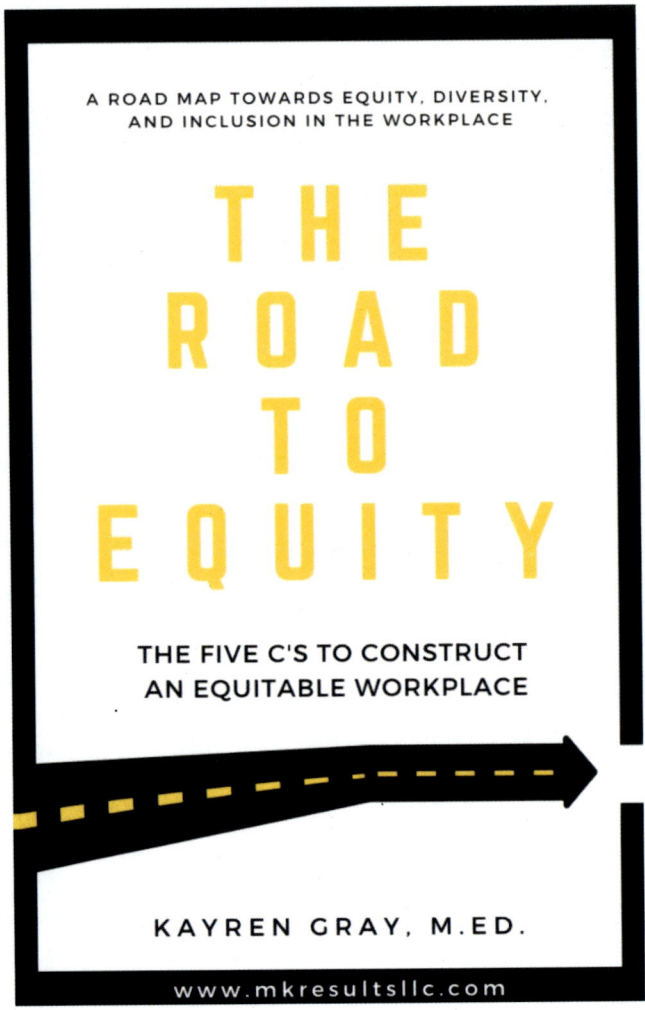

Available December 31, 2020

Made in the USA
Columbia, SC
10 June 2020